Healing Yourself
Understanding How Your MIND Can Heal Your BODY

Healing Yourself
Understanding How Your MIND Can Heal Your BODY

SHEILA PENNINGTON, Ph.D.

McGRAW-HILL RYERSON LIMITED
Toronto   Montreal   New York

Healing Yourself: Understanding How Your Mind Can Heal Your Body
© 1988 Centre for the Healing Arts Inc.

All rights reserved. No part of this publication may be reproduced, or transmitted in any form or by any means, or stored in a data base or retrieval system, without the prior written permission of the copyright holder.

This edition published in 1991 by
McGraw-Hill Ryerson Limited
300 Water Street
Whitby, Ontario L1N 9B6

1 2 3 4 5 6 7 8 9 0   D   0 9 8 7 6 5 4 3 2 1

Printed and bound in Canada

Care has been taken to trace the ownership of any copyright material contained in this text. The publishers will gladly take any information that will enable them to rectify any reference or credit in subsequent editions.

This book is not intended to replace the services of a physician. Any application of the recommendations set forth in the following pages is at the reader's discretion and sole risk.

Canadian Cataloging in Publication Data

Pennington, Sheila, date-
    Healing yourself

ISBN 0-07-549655-0 (bound)   0-07-551269-6

1. Mental healing. 2. Cancer—Psychological aspects.
3. Terminally ill—Case studies. I. Title

RZ400.P46 1988   615.8'51   C88-093592-8

In memory of my mother, Marion Haddow Catto, who taught me the meaning of human rights and personal dignity

To the six people interviewed for this book whose courage, struggle, and honesty are a source of inspiration and to all my clients who continue to teach me by sharing their mystery, agony, and beauty

CONTENTS

Preface ix
Acknowledgments x
Introduction xi
1 The Struggle Within 1
2 The Self-Healers 9
3 Journey to Health 31
4 Stage One: Awareness 39
5 Stage Two: Meaning 45
6 Stage Three: Choice 55
7 Stage Four: Will 61
8 Stage Five: Responsibility 67
9 Stage Six: Strategies 73
10 Stage Seven: Change 85
11 Examining the Healing Path 91
12 The Connection Between Mind and Body 123
13 Demystifying Healing 147
14 Healing Yourself: Part One 171
15 Healing Yourself: Part Two 203
16 Revitalization 237
Appendix 257
References 265

PREFACE

This book is about life renewal: a dynamic, inner change that affects one's quality and style of living as well as one's physical health.

We have extensive information on helping people prepare for death, but helping ourselves to re-evaluate our lives for the purpose of survival is relatively unexplored territory.

How does it happen that some people diagnosed as terminally ill die, while others with the same diagnosis extend and even improve the quality of their lives and sometimes recover completely?

This question was the subject of scientific research for my doctoral dissertation, "Living or Dying: An Investigation of the Balance Point," and it is on this research that *Healing Yourself: Understanding How Your Mind Can Heal Your Body* is founded.

This book describes the life-extending and life-transforming patterns that emerged through a scientific investigation of the lives of six people who had been diagnosed with terminal cancer and given a predicted date of death. The remarkable and fascinating recoveries or journeys to health of some of my clients are also described.

My research purpose was to discover the psychological dynamics that tip the balance point from dying to living when one is confronted with a physician's diagnosis of "hopeless" that is based solely on one's physical condition.

Although the six people interviewed had been diagnosed as terminally ill, the outstanding results of their *actions* are relevant for any of us with any illness, whether *physical, emotional, or spiritual.* The ways in which they responded to their diagnoses dramatically affected their living or dying. Their examples provide us with a life-giving key—a key that opens the door to the potential we each posses for *confronting, listening to, and overcoming illness.* The open door introduces us to profound new vistas as we embark on a journey to health.

ACKNOWLEDGMENTS

Writing this book has been a joyful and challenging experience. I am grateful to the following people who have shared the experience with me.

My husband and friend, Ben Harrison, whose unceasing love and encouragement fuelled my creative energy and whose faith in my ability to write has been an inspiration.

My father, Charles E. Catto, for being an outstanding example of health and who at 86 still rides a slalom water ski!

My daughter Ann for her diligent editing of the first draft and her wonderful, enthusiastic comments.

Past client, now friend and colleague Marion Yates, for bringing me chicken soup and sharing her love and excitement.

Drs. John Weiser and Robert MacIntyre for their brilliance as professors and compassionate interaction with me.

Dr. Alexander Szatmari for helping me discover myself.

Dr. Bryn Waern for helping me heal my heart.

Dr. Verna Hunt and Jennifer Berry for their healing hands and encouragement of my natural healing processes.

Dr. Kentwell for believing in me and McGraw-Hill Ryerson.

Authors June Callwood and Bill Kilbourn for their reading of an early draft, constructive comments, and enthusiasm.

My editorial cohorts, Jane Champagne, Margaret McClintock, Jennifer Glossop, Betty Jane Corson, Rosalyn Steiner, chief editor Denise Schon, and her perceptive secretary, Jane Cain.

I give you all my heartfelt thanks.

INTRODUCTION

The theory that psychological factors influence the etiology and course of human cancer dates back at least to the time of Galen in A.D. 200. Throughout the centuries this theory has surfaced, sometimes gaining widespread support in medicine, and, at other times, receiving little notice. At the turn of this century the development of general anesthesia led medicine to such a high level of specialization and technology that any idea of psychological influence was almost eclipsed from medical literature.

In the 1940s the work of Franz Alexander and Flanders Dunbar began the psychosomatic medicine movement in the United States. However, these theories, and the research that supported them, were largely retrospective and correlational in nature and were generally dismissed by scientific medicine of the day. It was not until the late 1960s that early biofeedback researchers began to report on a phenomenon that may eventually revolutionize the practice of medicine. Laboratory subjects were able, as documented by biological technology, to mentally influence physiological processes that were previously thought to be "involuntary" or outside the conscious control of the human psyche. Such autonomic nervous system processes as heart rate, blood pressure, blood flow, and skin temperature were influenced by the subject's conscious thought processes. The limits of this phenomenon have not yet been defined.

When I first approached the field of oncology in the late 1960s, my colleagues and I began asking whether a cancer patient's mental and emotional resources could influence the course of the disease. Numerous investigators hypothesized that a person's psychological makeup allowed the breakdown of his or her body's host resistance to cancer. The mechanisms were not clearly understood, but the similarity of personality factors frequently observed in cancer patients led to the hypothesis that those personality factors had somehow participated in allowing the growth of cancer.

The question that still remained was whether those personality factors could be changed, and if they were, would they alter the outcome of the patient's disease. It was hard to ignore those patients that survived their "incurable" cancer. Even more striking was the unusual psychological makeup and attitude of those patients, particularly regarding their disease. Spontaneous remission is a term frequently used to describe the disappearance of cancer that cannot be attributed to medical treatment. As long as medicine has observed the disease of cancer, spontaneous remissions have apparently occurred. They are not frequent in cancer treatment, and too often are dismissed as accidents. Yet there is good scientific rationale for studying the unusual response to gain insight into the phenomenon. Medical scientists have extensively studied the biological factors of hundreds of documented reports of spontaneous remission to no avail. However, this phenomenon has almost entirely escaped psychological investigation.

Dr. Pennington's work is a significant contribution to the scanty literature that has turned to the psyche of the patient who experiences a "spontaneous" remission for its explanation. In my own experience with these extraordinary patients their remissions were anything but spontaneous. It generally took weeks, months, or years of persistent and courageous hope that their prognosis did not necessarily have to become a reality. The road was often a lonely, isolated journey in family and medical systems that often labeled the patient's refusal to accept the prognosis as neurotic, if not psychotic. One has to wonder if this lack of support could account in part for the infrequency of spontaneous remissions.

Healing Yourself: Understanding How Your Mind Can Heal Your Body offers something to all people facing a life-threatening illness that is too often missing: hope concerning the outcome of that illness. By documenting numerous patients who have experienced an unusual course of disease, Dr. Pennington creates a model whereby recovery can happen, even in the face of seemingly overwhelming statistics. This book brings spontaneous remission out of the wastebasket and provides a rationale that demystifies it. If it is not an accident of nature, then perhaps any patient can learn to mobilize his or her psychological resources in the fight against disease. The path to health for many patients may now be one of support and enlightenment as society is informed of the possibility of the improbable.

A word of caution to those who may use the findings of Dr. Pennington in their own battle against illness. Too often patients with life-threatening illnesses have abandoned medical treatments that could aid their recovery because of their physician's pessimism or emotional insensitivity. Too often oncologists become jaded by their experience with death and lose hope themselves. This can certainly be detrimental to their patients' belief. However, there have always been those sensitive clinicians who have learned over years of treating diseases like cancer that the unexpected sometimes happens. They are able to remain hopeful in the face of serious illness, imbuing their patients with their optimism. Today there is a growing awareness in the field of oncology that a patient's attitude is important in the outcome of the illness. It may take considerable effort for patients to seek out those hope-enhancing physicians, but they are increasing in numbers. It is unfortunate that patients often reject good medical treatment when they dismiss a callous physician.

There are certainly those rare cases of recovery without medical intervention. In my experience, however, the number of patients who have survived a terminal prognosis have usually done so through their own courageous efforts and the support and resources of medicine. I sincerely believe that healing occurs best when both medicine and the psyche are brought to bear on a disease.

>Stephanie M. Simonton
>Little Rock, Arkansas
>January 1988

Healing Yourself
Understanding How Your MIND Can Heal Your BODY

1

THE STRUGGLE WITHIN

Two souls alas! are lodged within my breast, which struggle there for undivided reign. —Goethe

I work as a psychotherapist in Toronto, Ontario, and during the past few years, I have been seeing many clients with psychogenic illness—illness manifested by physical symptoms, but thought to originate in the mind, in emotional or psychological conflict. Working with such clients, I have become increasingly aware of a fundamental struggle occurring within them, within other clients, and at times within myself. In each case, two opposing forces seem to be wrestling: one represents growth and creativity, the other self-destruction. I believe this duality exists in all of us and has existed from the time of our beginning.

Internationally recognized psychologist Rollo May describes this struggle as "a primordial conflict, light triumphing over darkness, a conflict of good versus evil, 'yes' versus 'no,' order versus revolution." May believes this conflict to be "precisely the conflict that gave us consciousness in the first place" and that "this dialectic struggle is what makes human beings human."

The ancient Greeks deified these two conflicting forces; they named one Eros, the god of love; the other, Thanatos, the god of death. Eros represents our urge to create, achieve, and improve; it is the affirming, upward thrust of life. Thanatos represents a negative, downward, destructive impetus.

If you stop to think about it, you can probably recognize some form of this struggle within yourself. Most people have at some point in their lives felt so deeply frustrated and disappointed that they thought, however briefly, of lying down and giving up. Or they have felt that the solution to a problem, or the way out of a difficult relationship or situation, was beyond their reach.

My own life has included several such personal crises: a painful marital separation and divorce when I was thirty-six; the loss of a full-term, stillborn baby six years later; and a medical diagnosis of a prolapsed heart valve at age forty-four. At first, these experiences produced almost unbearable desolation. In each instance, I was aware of a struggle within myself, a choice to succumb to certain defeat or to find the will to struggle, grow, and create a new reality for myself.

I realized that by making a choice I was indicating my preference and that this necessarily demanded discarding, eliminating, or relinquishing other choices. Choice often involves conflict, and conflict is frequently painful. The pain of giving up old concepts and behavior, however, *can* lead to the birth of new understanding. The release of old patterns of behavior can bring the dawning of a new way of life. It has been said that to die is to be reborn, that continual rebirth is the essence of living.

When I realized that my first marriage was disintegrating, I decided to seek help in the form of psychotherapy. My former husband came to a few sessions, but often he forgot his appointments or canceled them, and eventually he abandoned them. I could have used his actions as an excuse to not continue therapy, but I chose to continue and to give up my ingrained dependence on his decisions. By relinquishing an old pattern of behavior, I grew into a new understanding of myself.

I soon faced a crossroads in my life. One direction pointed to helpless acceptance ("There's nothing you can do about it, Sheila"), and thence to depression, unresolved anger, bitterness, and hopelessness. The other road led to a re-evaluation of my life and of my own worth. I realized that I *could* choose and that I *could* take action.

For example, when my ex-husband failed to send the monthly payments he had agreed to provide in exchange for the money from the sale of our home, I was encouraged by family and friends to accept the financial hardship and not upset myself. I chose not to follow this advice. It took almost ten years to obtain a court judgment against my former husband, but I learned and grew from the experience itself, increased my confidence in my own strength, and demonstrated to myself the impact I can have when I take action.

During my second marriage, when my baby arrived stillborn, I was again advised by family and friends simply to accept my loss. Learning to accept something beyond my control was extremely difficult, but has made me wiser. I did not, however, stop with acceptance. I discovered that my baby could possibly have been saved. I was in perfect health and the autopsy on the baby indicated nothing defective; I could have been hospitalized earlier, exploratory tests could have been taken; I could have been more assertive and asked for opinions from other doctors, any of which might have prevented my baby's death. My awareness was growing. I spent three months in therapy, exploring my feelings of guilt for becoming pregnant at forty-one and for living a stressful life. Reaching out to a therapist for help, letting myself be vulnerable and receptive, and experiencing my deep grief and loss added to both my personal and professional growth.

My decision to write this book is a result of my experience with the discouraging diagnosis of a prolapsed heart valve. Approximately ten years ago I began to have considerable pain in my chest. My physician suggested that I take some tranquilizers and the occasional sleeping pill and get more rest. I tried all three remedies and found no change in my condition except increasing pain. I was then referred to a heart specialist, a cardiologist, who gave me a battery of tests and exercises, and the final diagnosis—a prolapsed heart valve. He explained to me that the tissue of my mitral valve had become flabby and the valve was no longer opening and closing normally. This was causing the pain and an irregular heart rhythm. I was given a prescription for Inderal, which I was to take four times daily for the rest of my life. When I asked my doctor what I could do to help myself get better, he responded, "Absolutely nothing. You will probably eventually require open heart surgery and have your mitral valve replaced by a pig's valve, à la John Wayne. In the meantime, trust in the progress of medical science."

I was stunned and horrified. The diagnosis in itself was a shock, but the doctor's callous attitude and words wrenched from me all responsibility for the future health of my heart and left me feeling impotent and afraid. I decided I needed to go far away to be alone with these feelings, and to make sense of this event in my life. I packed my car, took Zip, my comforting and trusty dog, and drove out to Cape Cod for a week. My husband and children gave me their full support, which lessened any feelings of guilt I had for "deserting the ship." Ben said he would fly down at the end of the week and help me drive home.

I rented a little cottage on a deserted part of the beach. I walked for miles beside the ocean through beautiful sand dunes. I cried and cried, and even screamed in anguish and frustration. I felt too young and too alive to be "put out to pasture." Zip understood my feelings completely and, aside from rolling on a dead sea gull, was a marvelous companion. By the end of the week I had achieved some peace of mind and a tentative plan of action. I felt that, even though I might not be able to change the direction my health appeared to be taking, perhaps I could somehow stem the tide. I could try to understand how I had let my heart become damaged.

Upon my return to Toronto, I sought out a therapist who was also a nutritionist. Together we looked at some of the recent stresses in my life. I had not taken the time to realize how considerable these were. I had been taking legal action to claim child support from my first husband for the past few years, had been raising two teenage children on my own, had recently remarried and taken a stepson into my home, had had a stillborn baby girl, and was conducting a thriving psychotherapy practice. I realized I was not taking enough time for exercise, for socializing with friends, or for aesthetic enjoyment.

I decided to make some changes in my lifestyle. I gradually cut my practice by one-third and asked for more help around the house from Ben and our children. To help my body deal with stress, I took megadoses of vitamins and minerals, especially vitamins C and E. I soon weaned myself from the Inderal, which had been making me feel worse rather than better. I made time for exercise every day, fresh air, friends, entertainment, and made sure to take some time off every three months or so. I began to feel better.

It came as a surprise to notice a decrease in my chest pain and a gradual return of energy. I went on with my life, gradually learning to be grateful that my heart had warned me to change aspects of my lifestyle before something more serious happened. Approximately three years later, I was on the West Coast and went swimming, outside, in early April (it took me a long time to learn to take proper care of myself). A nasty cold resulted and it rapidly developed into bronchial pneumonia. Because I believe that it is wise to listen to medical opinion before making one's own decision, I visited the emergency department of the nearest hospital. I told the doctor about my prolapsed heart valve so that he would understand why my heartbeat was different from normal. Much to my surprise, he informed me that he was not picking up an abnormal heartbeat. A few weeks later I made an appointment with another doctor in British Columbia. He also did not find any abnormality. When I reached Toronto, I was examined by one of the city's leading heart specialists who gave me a clean bill of health, describing my heart as "perfectly normal and healthy."

Well! I was ecstatic! Of course there are always skeptics who don't really accept the notion of healing oneself. Some of my acquaintances said, "Oh, it must have been a misdiagnosis." This was, however, my heart, my pain, and my experience, and I knew and trusted what had happened to me. The three main indicators were that I was feeling much better, had more energy, and was not experiencing any chest pain. I *knew* that I had healed my heart. And why not? The valve is made of collagen, a protein that is a chief component of connective tissue—why shouldn't it heal? I had reduced the stress in my life, was nourishing myself in a healthy, productive way, and had no more chest pain. *Voilà!*

I thought, if I could do this for myself, what else could people be doing for themselves? Our bodies are a mystery of activity and efficiency; our potential for healing ourselves is enormous. The healing of my heart became the inspiration for this book.

2
THE SELF-HEALERS

> *We must awaken and stay awake, not by mechanical means, but by the constant expectation of the dawn.* —Thoreau

My personal experiences with illness and the medical profession have taught me to trust my own judgment and ability to heal myself in conjunction with medical opinion. Experiences concerning my health that appeared to be frightening and negative in the first instance have turned out to be extremely rewarding and fulfilling in the long run.

I have had a few anxious experiences with different gynecologists. Several times I was informed that I had cervical dysplasia, which means that abnormal cells had grown on or near my cervix. Each time, there were no symptoms, and the dysplasia was detected by a Pap smear. The first time I was in my twenties and completely doctor-dependent: it would never have crossed my mind to question any statement made by a doctor. In my family and in those of most of my friends, one was quite simply discouraged from questioning the verity of religious or medical dogma. The doctor's dictum was that my cervix should be cauterized, a procedure in which abnormal tissue is destroyed by the application of an electrically heated instrument. This treatment was somewhat painful, definitely uncomfortable, and unpleasant: I did not like the smell of my tissues burning.

At the age of thirty-five I was informed by my gynecologist that it would be necessary for me to have a conization on my cervix. My gynecologist asked which week I would like to have a hospital bed reserved for me. Conization is a surgical procedure done under general anesthesia. I was nervous about the idea and decided to get a second opinion. The next gynecologist I consulted asked me if I cared about the appearance of my cervix. I replied that I really didn't, as long as it was healthy. He stated that it was perfectly healthy and that any surgery would be solely for cosmetic reasons. I was relieved by and grateful for this information but angry with my first gynecologist. When I returned to him armed with the second opinion, he responded sheepishly that he had not really said the operation was imperative. Needless to say, I did not have the operation and found another gynecologist.

Twice since then I have been informed that I have had a recurrence of cervical dysplasia. These times, being more mature and better informed, I have requested that we wait six months before applying any medical treatment. Both times, I returned after six months for another Pap smear. My gynecologist and I were both pleasantly surprised to find that the smears produced negative results; in other words, I was clear. I was informed that out of fifteen women who had returned for the second test, I was the only one whose test results were healthy. What I had done in the interim was to take better care of myself in every respect and to visualize my cervical cells becoming healthy.

Around this time, my husband Ben noticed blood in his urine. He had had a recurring bladder infection two or three times a year for several years. Feelings of complete exhaustion would be followed by pain in his groin and excruciating pain when urinating, followed by blood. Each time the doctor would examine Ben's urine, confirm that he had an infection, and prescribe a drug. Ben would take the drug for about thirty days, after which time all symptoms would be gone. Then, in a few months, they would reappear. Finally he was sent to a urologist. The urologist performed a cystoscopy, using a tubelike instrument with a light in it, to dilate and examine Ben's urethra. He found evidence of scar tissue caused, he assumed, by an old injury. Ben recalled the pain he had from falling down an open stairwell and also from a severe football injury to the groin. The infection was being caused by the scar tissue blocking the urethra and causing the urine to back up in the bladder. The bladder acted as a pool in which infection could develop—infection that could make its way to the kidneys and cause serious damage.

The doctor thought that the dilation might in itself cause the tissue to be flushed out. In six weeks, however, the infection recurred and Ben was examined again. This time the urologist said that the only way to prevent recurrence of the infection was for Ben to have surgery. The only possible alternative to surgery, he said, would be for Ben to come in every six weeks to have his urethra stretched. He suggested a date for the operation within the next few days.

The operation would be a two-stage process involving the removal of the scarred portion of the urethra, a graft, and the installation of a shunt into the penis to redirect the urine. This would be followed by a second surgical procedure six months later to remove the shunt. Ben did not like the two choices he had been given, and did not know what to do.

He and I discussed the possibility of choosing neither and, instead, using his mind and his inner eye to heal himself. Ben decided to visualize his urine washing away the scar tissue. Every time he urinated, he visualized the free flow of his urine and, following urination, he always drank a glass of water. He has practiced this routine faithfully and the infection has never returned. It has been seven years since he decided against having the recommended surgery and he has had no problems, taken no drugs, and is eternally grateful for trying a healing method different from that advised by his doctor.

Such personal experiences encouraged me to learn more about self-healing. I became increasingly interested in seeing clients with health-related problems. One of them, Suzanne, began psychotherapy with me when she was told by her doctor that she required a hysterectomy. Through therapy and by using nonmedical self-healing methods such as meditation and visualization, she was able to clear herself of uterine cancer without undergoing surgery and has remained active and healthy for the past five years.

Another client, Sally, had anorexia nervosa, a disease that often terminates in death by starvation. Sally was fourteen years old, stood five feet, six inches tall, and weighed sixty pounds. She had been told by four different doctors that she would probably die. I asked her for her own diagnosis: she said she was going to live. Together, through individual and family psychotherapy, we agreed to fulfill her diagnosis. Sally has been back at school for seven years, her menses have returned, and she now weighs 140 pounds. Caring, trust, and an awareness of choice, will, responsibility, and action had proved to be the agents for life-affirming change.

One of my clients, Tom, came for psychotherapy because he had been feeling anxious and tired and had developed a recurring rash on his face and neck. Together we discovered that he wasn't "facing" up to the fact that when he allowed his life to become overstressed the rash became redder and more angry looking. Tom was finally able to prioritize his time to include more rest and recreation. As he reduced his stress level, his rash gradually receded.

Another client, Gillian, found from time to time that she experienced a partial loss of vision. By examining the patterns in her life, she realized that this loss occurred after particularly upsetting experiences. She had been repressing her emotional responses. As she increased her understanding of hurt and anger and learned to express them in acceptable ways, she experienced less and less loss of vision. She realized she had been "blind" with anger.

Tim, a child client, had several disfiguring warts on his hands and some on his feet. His mother and he had unsuccessfully tried various medications in an effort to get rid of them. I taught Tim how to relax, to breathe more deeply, and to imagine himself having the power and the desire to "will" away his warts. Tim became very excited when the first one began to diminish in size. When I last saw Tim he had only one wart left.

Cheryl had dreamed of becoming a professional dancer, and she was heartbroken when she cracked a bone in her foot that could not be healed well enough to allow her to dance properly. Although she lacked faith in her intellectual abilities, she went back to school to study nutrition and surprised herself with her success and enjoyment. Acceptance of her impairment allowed her to develop untapped potential and power.

Kathie was diagnosed with cancer of the uterus and had a hysterectomy. The cancer reappeared in her breast and she had a mastectomy. She believed that her cancer would continue to reappear if she didn't get her life together. She acknowledged she was "falling apart." Along with the disintegration of her body her relationships with friends and family were also deteriorating. Kathie physically felt the emptiness of her life where her uterus had been. She decided to take up bellydancing and has never looked back. Bellydancing is a strenuous activity; she now performs and teaches it. For five years there has been no further sign of cancer, her personal relationships are restored, and her body and spirit indicate healthy energy.

Life renewal is a startling concept. When we are ill, we do not think of ourselves as self-healers. Instead, we head for the medicine cabinet or to a doctor's office. Modern medicine has taught us to perceive ourselves as objects for treatment. Generally speaking, medical science perceives human beings as aggregations of body parts rather than as whole persons. Powers of self-healing have been ignored: spiritual and emotional factors in health have been disregarded and any nonmedical healing has for the most part been dismissed.

But our thoughts and feelings *do* affect our health. This fact has been confirmed by many scientific studies. There is conclusive evidence that prolonged stress can inhibit the immune system. But the fact that the mind can *relieve* illness as well as *create* illness is still ignored.

The ways in which our individual beliefs, attitudes,

relationships, and environments improve our health and halt disease have been largely disregarded by the medical profession and by us. We have not yet recognized the exciting potential of our own capabilities for self-healing. Instead we place all our confidence in medical treatment. And when medical intervention fails to halt or turn around a debilitating disease, we consider the situation to be hopeless. And if we receive a so-called terminal diagnosis, we reach a literal **dead** end. Most individuals accept such a diagnosis and die within a year of the date predicted by their doctors.

There are those, however, who do not die, but go on to live full and productive lives. If I was able to restore my heart to healthy functioning after having been told by expert physicians that there was nothing I could do, what might people who are given far more serious prognoses be able to do for themselves? The experience of healing myself reinforced my belief in the potential power we have for change.

I remembered Einstein's assertion that energy and matter are interchangeable. Suppose my mind creates a thought, an electrical impulse—energy that is then transmitted to my body, to matter. Why couldn't this "matter" change? It's only tissue. My heart valve is composed of connective tissue and it healed. A figurative far off pinpoint of light began to glimmer. I started my journey toward that light by embarking on the research upon which this book is based. Because psychology is both an art and a science, I wanted to approach this investigation with the forging tools of both. It was important that I be both subjective and objective; as a parent is with a child, as a therapist is with a client. For this, the central ingredients are compassion and clarity.

Only those who have received a diagnosis predicting their death can really know what this experience means to them, and it seemed apparent that the best way for me to obtain information about their experiences was neither to ask their doctors, nor their family and friends, but them. My intent was to discover whether their illnesses had carried a meaning for them and, if so, how this meaning had manifested itself in their subsequent attitudes and actions. It was my hope that my investigation would contribute new knowledge to the matrix of disease, stress, loss, and conflict and would encourage the development of strategies for self-healing and the prevention of illness.

☐ THE PEOPLE

The criteria I used for selecting the six individuals who were to become participants in my research were that they had been medically diagnosed as terminally ill, that their doctors had predicted the approximate date of their death, and that they had outlived that date by at least two years.

The first person I heard about was Gregory Bateson, the American anthropologist. I was informed that he had gone to Esalen to die following a diagnosis of terminal lung cancer and was still living. Esalen is a humanist center for learning and psychological advancement located on the shore of the Pacific Ocean near Big Sur, California. It is a temporal paradise in terms of intellectual stimulation, spectacular natural beauty, and honest, human interaction. Bateson chose to spend the last years of his life in this atmosphere, living in the house constructed by Fritz Perls, the father of Gestalt psychology. This unusual house is safely nestled in the arms of nature. The view from the porch is breathtaking: on one side is the sheer beauty of the mountains; on the other side is a precipitous drop to the ocean.

I was convinced that someone of the stature of Gregory Bateson would never consent to be interviewed by me, but he not only agreed, he indicated considerable interest in my endeavor. In April 1980 I visited him at Esalen.

☐ *Gregory Bateson*

Gregory Bateson was born in 1904, the son of William Bateson, a leading British biologist and a pioneering geneticist. An internationally renowned anthropologist, professor, and scientist, author of *Steps to an Ecology of Mind* and *Mind and Nature: A Necessary Unity*, and the former husband of world-famous anthropologist Margaret Mead, Bateson was diagnosed with lung cancer in January 1978. His physician was unable to operate because of the location of the cancer and predicted that Bateson's death would be imminent: in a week or a month at most. At one point, Bateson said, his family was told not to expect to see him alive after his diagnostic surgery. He died two and a half years later, not of cancer but of respiratory disorders. Before his death, he made an important contribution through his teaching, writing, and thought-provoking criticism of the medical profession.

My interview with Bateson was warm and stimulating. At first he found it difficult to share his feelings, but ultimately he seemed grateful to have an opportunity to share his pessimism, boredom, and anger. He was tired, accepting of death, and too discouraged to want to live longer. He had not resolved his anger. He felt that his parents had scripted him to become a successful academic, a script he had fulfilled. On the other hand, his brother had protested academia by committing suicide under a statue of Eros. Bateson felt caught between these two positions: he wanted to please his parents but resented carrying the burden of his past on his back.

In speaking with him, he pointed out that, if a collection of parts is to form a whole, and if that whole is to be a *living* system, a system of communication—of connection—between the parts is required. Bateson viewed the mind-body as a communication system, capable of generating, receiving, interpreting, and responding to messages—and of sending out new messages. If a person is a communication system, then disease is a message within and to that system: what we call disease is the manifestation of mislaid or interrupted messages.

Bateson did not believe that a pill, a word, a diagnosis, a major operation, or a cancer is its own sufficient definition; each of these must be seen in context. There are patients who do not die even though their doctors told them their condition was terminal. Does this mean that established medicine has failed? Bateson believed that the context of every medical transaction includes both the thinking of the doctor as he administers to the patient and the corresponding thinking of the patient. Bateson's conviction was that "the structure of medical services, of the doctor's thought and action, and the structure of the patient's thought and physiology should fit together. What the doctor believes him- or herself to be should be compatible with what the doctor believes his or her patient to be."

He suggested that doctors do not in general make good patients because of their deep belief in "the philosophy of materialistic medicine." Bateson was, from the medical profession's point of view, a "successful patient," in that he recovered. He felt this was ironic, since he recovered by taking an unorthodox approach to his healing and by maintaining his own independent philosophy about health.

After my visit to Bateson, I went to the Simonton Cancer Counselling and Research Center, then located in Fort Worth, Texas, in order to familiarize myself with its innovative form of therapy and also to demystify some of the rumors about unconventional healing techniques. Carl Simonton and Stephanie Matthews-Simonton are leading practitioners in the field of psychological causes and treatment of cancer. Carl, the medical director of the center, is a radiation oncologist, a physician specializing in the treatment of cancer. Stephanie was director of the counseling program and is trained in psychology. Most of their patients have received a "medically incurable" diagnosis from their doctors and, according to national cancer statistics, have an average life expectancy of one year. There I met a man who had been in therapy with the Simontons. This man, whom I'll call Dean Bishop, had been given a terminal diagnosis of multiple myeloma, a rapidly growing form of cancer of the bone marrow, three years earlier. At the time I met him, his doctors could discover no sign of the disease. He agreed to be interviewed.

☐ Dean Bishop

Dean Bishop is a physicist, a pilot, a businessman, and a family man. In 1975, at the age of sixty-three, he was told he had cancer.

This diagnosis followed a yearly physical examination given to all pilots. Bishop's blood tests showed a high total protein, and the blood, when broken down by electrophoresis, showed a high monoclonal peak indicative of cancer of the bone marrow. Bishop was then given bone scans, which were negative. A hematologist did a bone-marrow biopsy and, because of the presence of a large number of immature cells, concluded that Bishop had multiple myeloma. At the time, it was predicted that he would suffer a very painful death within two years. Twelve years later he is alive and well with absolutely no sign of cancer.

Until his diagnosis, Bishop had been a hard-nosed businessman, mainly interested in making money and getting ahead—a lifestyle, he realizes now, that affected his relationships and his health in a destructive way. For some time he had felt a dichotomy within himself, a struggle between negativity and affirmation. He had had problems with his children as they were growing up, and these differences continued after he received his terminal diagnosis. He and his wife had also had problems with their relationship.

At the time of the diagnosis and during the preceding two years, Bishop had experienced significant personal and business losses; the businesses had taken him twenty-five years to build up. He was selling them. His children were choosing their own directions in life, and he viewed this as a loss: "They were departing from the ways in which I had them programmed." He said his children did not seem to recognize that he knew what was best for them. Bishop was then unaware of his rigidity in personal relationships. Another loss was the sale of the family home where they had lived for twenty-five years. Both his parents had died and there were problems with inheritance taxes. He felt a lack of challenge without his business commitments and was increasingly tired.

One of the hardest blows Bishop suffered was having someone else limit the length of time he had left to live. "It was almost something I couldn't stand," he said. He finally reclaimed his life by dramatically changing his style of living. He de-emphasized monetary aspects and gave priority to relationships. He worked extremely hard in psychotherapy and was exhilarated to discover how he had contributed to his illness and how he could help recover his health.

I found interviewing this man an emotional experience. I was impressed that a person in his sixties could change so totally and develop such a thoughtful and expressive philosophy of life. His sensitivity, gentleness, and openness were quite remarkable.

From Texas I continued out to the West Coast to visit my thesis chairman, John Weiser, who was on sabbatical at Inverness, California. He had met a psychologist, whom I'll call Jim Searle, who had been given a terminal diagnosis several years earlier. He, too, agreed to be interviewed.

☐ Jim Searle

Jim Searle was a clinical psychologist and professor. In 1975, aged fifty-three, he was diagnosed with hypernephroma (renal cell carcinoma), a malignant tumor of the kidney cells, which had spread via the bloodstream and appeared as a secondary growth in one of his lungs. Given less than two years to live, he survived for six.

Following his first two bouts with cancer, Searle developed it next in his jaw, and finally in his wrist. The cancer would appear to be gone and would then reappear.

Apparently Searle had tried to call me to cancel his interview, saying that he felt weak and discouraged and felt like "running" from the interview. When I arrived at his office he again tried to put me off. At the beginning of the interview he was tired, pale, and disconsolate; however, by its conclusion his color was good, he felt energized and renewed. He thanked me for my persistence and understanding.

The hardest thing for Searle was to learn the importance of honesty in human relationships. Being honest was critical for him; he felt that his lack of honesty with himself and others had interfered with his life and allowed cancer to grow. Jim Searle died in August 1981.

On my return to Toronto, a friend told me of a biofeedback therapist, whom I'll call Ann Latimer, who had outlived her predicted date of death. She had been given a terminal diagnosis of lymphosarcoma. Latimer, too, consented to be interviewed.

☐ Ann Latimer

Ann Latimer, a woman of amazing pluck and courage, fought strongly for the right to make decisions about her own body. She was diagnosed with lymphosarcoma in 1975 and was given one year to live. She died six years later from cancer at the age of sixty.

When, in 1975, Latimer discovered a lump in her breast, the first indication of lymphosarcoma, her surgeon wanted to perform a mastectomy immediately. She refused adamantly, insisted on a lumpectomy, and was hurt that the surgeon had not considered her feelings about the operation. In hospital, she was given preoperative medication and fell asleep. When she awoke, she realized with anger that her scheduled time for surgery had passed, that her doctor had been overbooked, and that she had needlessly taken preoperative medication. The doctor was angry with Latimer for being angry with him. He asked her to sign the consent form again, saying it wasn't quite right. As Latimer was about to sign, she noticed "mastectomy" written on it and refused to sign. Angry at his deception, she threatened to leave the hospital and go elsewhere. She crossed out the word mastectomy and wrote that under no circumstances would she consent to anything other than a lumpectomy. Latimer had a nurse witness her signature and stated that if the doctor did more than remove the lump, she would sue him. The lumpectomy was done and it made "an awful scar, very long, with a lot of little knobs on it."

Her own general practitioner told her that she had made an impact on the hospital personnel; that everyone knew about her case, because normally no one would dare to speak to a surgeon the way she had.

A year later Latimer's doctors discovered a large blockage in her bowel and recommended a colostomy. (A colostomy is a surgical operation in which a part of the colon is brought through the abdominal wall and opened to drain the intestine. An appliance is worn over the colostomy opening to prevent soiling.) Latimer was informed that if she did not have the operation, her bowels might not work at all. She refused to consent to the colostomy, opting for removal of the blockage only. The doctor went ahead with this requested surgery after expressing his belief that it would not be enough to keep her alive and that she would be dead by the end of the summer. She recovered, however, and became as fit as she had ever been in her life.

Latimer had no further problems with her bowel. Her life was content and without medical problems until two years later when she began to suffer excruciating pain in her neck vertebrae. X rays indicated a return of cancer, and she was given radiation. The side effects of the radiation emerged gradually. She lost weight and lost strength in her left arm. Her doctors said that the tingling in her arm had nothing to do with the radiation, that it must be the result of osteoarthritis. However, the resident physician who read her file said that the radiation she had been given had been directed a little too far to the left; Latimer felt that this gave some justification for her insistence that the problems with her arm were related to her radiation therapy. The radiation also affected her throat, and she had trouble eating. No one had informed her that these symptoms might be side effects of the radiation.

I felt a warm affection for Ann Latimer. She had not realized that she had so much to say, that her experience was so rich that she could help others by sharing what she had learned. This made her feel happy and purposeful in contrast to her depression when the interview began.

Then, right on my doorstep at the Ontario Institute for Studies in Education, where I was undertaking my doctorate, I was introduced to Doug Scott, a doctoral student in adult education and now a consultant, who had been diagnosed with skin cancer.

☐ Doug Scott

In February 1976 Doug Scott, forty-five, was diagnosed with malignant melanoma in a growing skin lesion on his back. Later that same year a tumor was discovered in his lung, and he was told that he had less than two years to live. He is still alive, in excellent health, with no sign of cancer.

Born in Bristol, England, Scott was brought to Canada by his parents when he was six months old. He was the middle child, with a brother one year older and a sister four years younger. When his mother was pregnant with Scott, she had toxemia and was hospitalized for the last four months of her pregnancy. Neither she nor the doctor expected the baby Scott to live, so perhaps he had struggled with hopelessness even in that threatened prebirth environment. When he was born, however, he was apparently healthy and beautiful—a surprise to everyone.

Scott grew up to be exceptionally nonsocial, enjoying independent activities, the unconventional, and taking his own direction. Scott believes that he has unusual insight and rare perception and has had this belief confirmed by others. On the other hand, his lack of role models from whom to learn emotional expression, when added to his own psychological nature, led him, as a child and later as an adult, to hold back and internalize his feelings.

Scott realizes now that he was raised in the "fine Scottish tradition," by which he means the philosophy that in this world you have to look after yourself. During the process of his illness and his healing he became aware of a sturdy Scottish strength within himself. He felt he inherited this strength from his father, who gave him a very positive message when he was in hospital for lung surgery: "Remember you are a Scott; we all pull through these tough times and we have the kind of strength and ruggedness that goes along with the clan, so you're going to be all right."

A friend of Scott's, a behavioral scientist, has influenced him deeply. When Scott told him of the diagnosis, his friend put his arms around him and said he felt Scott had what it takes to make it through, that he had a sense Scott would be okay. This reinforced his father's words and was a powerful positive expectation from someone very important to him.

The changes in Scott's demeanor during our interview seemed to parallel the changes he had made in his attitude and approach to life. As he described the process of his recovery, his voice changed from a depressed monotone to a voice that sounded very much alive. His appearance changed as he compared his experience before his diagnosis, when he was feeling helpless and trapped, to his present state of health, when his attitude changed to one of hope and action. Change seemed to come from within: as he became more aware of choice, will, and responsibility, he found the resources to make dramatic changes in his life.

Scott informed me in June 1981 that at his last medical examination, to the surprise of his doctor and himself, his chest X ray indicated that he had regenerated the rib that had been removed for lung surgery.

And last, but by no means least, I heard about Dr. Hans Selye, a Canadian and the international authority on stress. I had been reading his books on stress and had found out that he, too, had been given a terminal diagnosis. It was difficult to obtain an interview with Selye because of his extremely busy schedule, including teaching, research, lectures, and travel, but when I informed him of the nature of my research, he encouraged me by becoming a participant. I interviewed him in the autumn of 1979.

☐ Hans Selye

A world-renowned scientist, endocrinologist, professor, and author, Hans Selye was regarded as the father of theories on stress. As an eighteen-year-old medical student in Prague, he asked himself, "Why are sick people all so alike? Is there a syndrome of simply being sick?" He came to North America in 1930 on a Rockefeller grant, in search of an answer, and by 1932 was at work in Montreal, first at McGill University and then at the Université de Montréal. In 1945 he founded the Institute of Experimental Medicine and Surgery at the University of Montreal,

Quebec, and, in 1977, he established the International Institute of Stress (which he directed until his death in 1982). Formulated in the 1920s but not formally recognized until the mid-1950s, his conception of the link between stress and illness ultimately gained him world-wide status as an authority on stress-related disease. He held doctorates in philosophy and science, as well as medicine, and had been made a Companion of the Order of Canada, the country's highest honor. Selye wrote thirty-eight books, which have been translated into thirty-four languages. He gave lectures on stress in nine languages.

In 1973 Selye was diagnosed as having a normally fatal cancer, a histiocytic reticular sarcoma (a nodule in the lymph node), under the skin on one of his thighs. He researched this cancer and discovered that it was vicious and rapid spreading, that it almost always killed within a year, and that, in his own words, "There is no case of recovery recorded anywhere in the medical literature under any conditions whatsoever." Even when the tumor is cut out and radiation is used, the sarcoma puts out little metastases all over the body and, sooner or later, the cancer always reappears. Selye refused to retreat from life in desperation. He immediately underwent surgery and cobalt therapy, but refused to have chemotherapy. When he insisted on being informed of his chances for a lasting recovery, his doctors told him that it was impossible for him to survive more than one year. Although he knew it would take a great amount of discipline, Selye determined to continue living his life fully and immersed himself in what he most enjoyed—his work.

Selye recovered from cancer and lived eight years longer than expected. He died in 1982 of a heart attack. He felt that his recovery was assisted by motivation, attitude, and creative productivity. Selye was a man of great vision. I believe that someday he

BIOGRAPHICAL DATA OF PARTICIPANTS

PARTICIPANTS	DEAN BISHOP	JIM SEARLE	GREGORY BATESON	ANN LATIMER	DOUG SCOTT	HANS SELYE
How first discovered	Routine physical Electrophoresis of blood serum and bone marrow biopsy	Blood & urine nephrectomy Routine chest X ray	Spitting blood	Lump in breast	Growing skin lesion on back	Nodule in lymph node in leg
Date of first diagnosis	February 1975 Drs. Blide, Halden and Alexanian	1975	January 1978 Dr. C. McCormick	April 1975 Dr. Woolnough Dr. Provan	Feb. 1976 Dr. J. Starr	1973 Dr. Tabah
Predicted death date	Less than two years—Feb. 1977	1977	January 1978	1976	August 1979	1974
Natural death date	Still living	August 1981	July 1980	July 1981	Still living	1982
Age at diagnosis	63	47	73	54	45	66
Present age – 1987	75				57	

Medical name of disease	Multiple myeloma, malignant tumor of bone marrow	Hypernephroma, kidney cell cancer Lung cancer	Lung cancer	Lymphosarcoma	Melanocarcinoma, malignant melanoma	Histiocytic reticular sarcoma
Medical treatment	Three IV injections of chemotherapy over 3-week period	Surgery Radiation Chemotherapy Female hormone treatment recommended	Diagnostic surgery No removal of tissue	Radiation Chemotherapy	Surgery February 1978 January 1979	Surgery Radiation
Comments on treatment	Chose to discontinue chemotherapy	Rejected hormone treatment, surgery and chemotherapy	Carcinoma too large to remove without risk of hemorrhage	Not appreciative	Orthodox medicine helpful, also alternative therapies	Rejected chemotherapy
Recurrence	None	1977 – tumor in jaw 1978 – wrist cancer	None	May 1976 – colon 1978 – vertebra 1979 – urethra	Secondary tumor, left lung, Dec. 1978	None
Present health	Very good				Excellent	
Profession	Physicist and businessman	Clinical psychologist, professor	Professor, scientist, and author	Biofeedback therapist	Staff development and organizational consultant	Scientist, endocrinolist, and author

will be hailed as a revolutionary influence on health and illness, that medical treatment of symptoms will be overshadowed by preventive use of his theories on the effects of stress.

My interview with Selye had a profound affect on my thinking. He was the first, to my knowledge, to point to the fact that all persons diagnosed with disease have one thing in common—a depressed immune system. This seminal idea sprouts questions about the nature and effect of the immune system on illness and recovery and encourages us to seek further for the reasons why some people who are exposed to cancer-causing factors, Aids, flu, and other diseases do not develop the disease while others do.

Selye helped me to realize the importance of the research I was undertaking and the impact that any theory I might develop from my interviews could have on future health and well-being. He informed me that I had an ethical and moral responsibility to publish my findings.

□ 3
JOURNEY TO HEALTH

The search for one's own being, the discovery of the life one needs to live, can be one of the strongest weapons against disease.
—Lawrence LeShan

Up to the completion of the interviews, my search into the realms of illness and health had been primarily subjective. I was thrilled and amazed by the information shared with me. It was now imperative for me to step back and analyze objectively the material I had gathered.

I spent the next twelve months analyzing the interviews, which when transcribed ran to 256 typewritten pages. This process involved a systematic study of the data to find underlying patterns of experience.

These patterns, or themes, provided the framework for the construction of a general theory. The central core or essence of this theory is that each individual discovers his or her own path to health and that these paths have seven distinct stages in common. (For the interested reader, a description of the methods used in my analysis of the data and of the steps through which I discovered my general theory is given in the Appendix.)

☐ THEMES

The following twelve themes describing their experience of a terminal diagnosis were representative of those interviewed:

1. The awareness of the struggle between wanting to live and wanting to give up. This life-death struggle was described as a dichotomy within each person—as two differing views, as a choice between dying and living, and as two warring forces. Sometimes the struggle was recognized consciously and sometimes unconsciously in dreams. The life-death pull made the six participants in my study focus on their values.

2. The awareness of the need for identification with a higher power or force. The theme of a larger power evolved from the concept of identification with, or the loss of identification with, a sensé of something bigger than oneself—for example, the beauty, wisdom, and laws of nature, God, the universal unconscious, fate, an inner core, or the infinite.

3. The meaning of the diagnosis, including acceptance and nonacceptance. Their diagnoses

shocked these people into questioning life-and-death issues, such as the implications of the diagnosis, the direction their lives had been taking, and how to live in the time left. They confronted their fear of death and realized that in order to live they would have to make considerable changes in their style of living. In questioning their desire to live, they were able to get in touch with their feelings and discover what they really wanted from life.

4 The existence of choice as an option in determining a direction toward health or illness. The awareness that a choice between life and death was a possibility resonated strongly. The choice to live meant a change in attitude, beliefs, and lifestyle and led to joy, pleasure, appreciation of beauty, responsible action for oneself and in relationship to others, and an affirmation of life in terms of doing what one wants to do and sharing with others.

5 Will as a powerful force that directs action. The participants equated loss of will with death. The shock of the terminal diagnosis forced on them the awareness of the will to live. The components of will included resolve, determination, motivation, intention, and action. This active process also incorporated challenge, purpose, survival, strength, and fight.

6 The influence that one's beliefs and attitudes have on health. This theme centered on the participants' awareness that their emotional state and attitude had affected their health dramatically. Their fatalistic and pessimistic attitudes changed to a belief in the inherent wisdom of the body, in the wisdom of nature, and in their own inner resources. Hope, faith,

and self-worth were all factors in this theme.

7   The importance of taking individual responsibility for health. These people gradually learned to accept a measure of responsibility for getting sick. Responsibility for getting well included taking charge of their lives, being responsible for their bodies and their feelings, handling stress productively, and coming to terms with their mortality.

8   The creation of purpose and challenge. The diagnoses were instrumental in helping the participants to focus on what they wanted to do with the rest of their lives. Success in doing what they wanted would give them a purpose and provide them with a source of pleasure. They felt challenged to fulfill their potential and to contribute to humanity.

9   The development of strategies for survival and health maintenance. By strategies I mean the effective actions taken by these people in order to extend and increase the quality of their lives. Strategies used by all were exercise, different forms of meditation, and humor. These and other strategies will be described in a later chapter.

10 The importance and influence of relationships. The influence of others and the need to give and receive support were pervasive themes. Each person had found some significant other person who had made him or her feel special at one time or another.

11 The change that actually took place in their lives. The diagnosis itself delivered a powerful message: "change or else." Change became a life-or-death issue. Refusal to change came to be seen as a factor in getting sick. Change be-

came evident in attitudes, beliefs, action and lifestyle.

12. The psychological components of illness. All the participants felt that their illnesses had been caused, in part, by their own thoughts and that their recovery was aided by their thoughts. The experience of loss, a history of internalizing feelings prior to the onset of illness, and tumor regression resulting from motivation were recurring themes.

THE HEALING PATH

Throughout the process of analysis, I was hoping to find a pattern of behavior leading to change. As I considered the twelve themes, I became aware of a "will to action" running through the whole process much like a central artery. This synthesis of heart, mind, body, and spirit led each participant to an evolution of being, to a qualitatively different way of life. In the course of this evolution, this process of becoming, changes occurred. The individuals were emotionally, physically, socially, and spiritually different from the way they had been.

This "will to action" could also be described as personal power or agency. *Agency* is defined in *Webster's Third New International Dictionary* as "a person or thing through which power is exerted or an end is achieved." The individuals participating in this study achieved *the greatest possible improvement in their well-being in terms of extending and improving their quality of life.* They describe a pattern of behavior that explains their healing—their process of change from illness to health.

This power or agency was expressed in action by a

pattern that emerged as seven distinct stages. The stages seemed to form a path of stepping-stones from hopelessness and despair to health or wellness. Consequently I have named this the Healing Path or Personal Agency.

The usual response to a terminal diagnosis is horror, fear, hopelessness, and death. But as many have found, it is possible to choose an alternative approach to terminal disease. By following this route, this Healing Path, it is possible to redirect the journey away from disease and toward renewed life and health.

Each of the six participants underwent a similar process. Their journey to health passed through seven distinct stages, and as they progressed through them they revitalized and synthesized their mind, body, and spirit. They did not all change in the same manner, but they did all reverse the direction of their journey by living at least two years beyond their predicted date of death, and all improved their quality of life; two of them completely recovered their health.

These seven stages are essential to progression along the Healing Path: they constitute its structure. Each stage is necessary and contingent upon the others. They do not necessarily happen in successive order but reinforce each other in a kind of spiral effect. The beginning of the process is a terminal diagnosis. For each person the diagnosis created a crisis, which in turn ultimately triggered a process of life affirmation—a process that demanded change and, for three of the six participants, resulted in fundamental ongoing change.

The stages illustrate how the meaning that the participants attributed to their illness affected their attitudes and actions and enabled them to structure their experience of life in a manner that influenced the duration and quality of their lives.

The stages of the Healing Path are sometimes experienced consciously and often unconsciously. They may be perceived and understood after or at the same time as they are experienced. If the stages are understood beforehand, they may be brought about by conscious intention.

The seven stages of the Healing Path are (1) awareness, (2) meaning, (3) choice, (4) will, (5) responsibility, (6) strategies, and (7) change.

It appears that will is the fulcrum or central stepping stone of the Healing Path. The first three stages—awareness, meaning, and choice—are essentially psychological. The latter three stages—responsibility, strategies, and change—are more social, more related to environment. Will is action. The development of will results from the first three stages. The act of will or will in action is the essence of the latter three stages. If the awareness of the will to live is not transformed into active responsibility for living, then there is a tendency toward dependency, apathy, hopelessness, and ultimately death.

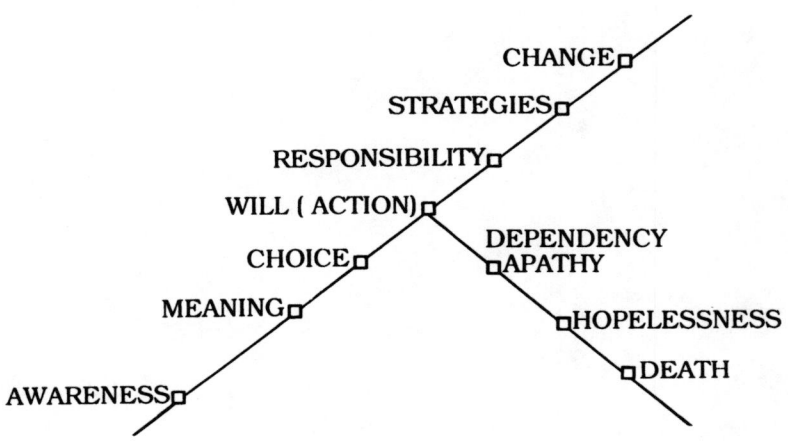

In the following chapters we will look at each of these stages in detail and examine how each of the individuals I interviewed found and followed the Healing Path.

4
STAGE ONE: AWARENESS

Persons are individuals who transcend their merely organic individuality in conscious participation. —Julian Huxley

The first step on the Healing Path is awareness: self-awareness and awareness in relation to others. This is the foundation for the other stages leading to change. Awareness, like awakening, occurs for individuals in different ways. It appears to be part of an evolving consciousness that creates sometimes abrupt but lasting change in attitudes and behavior.

There are three outstanding elements to the stage of awareness: (1) shock, (2) acceptance or nonacceptance of the medical diagnosis, and (3) confrontation of the life-death struggle—one of the crossroads on the journey to health.

☐ *1. Shock* It is shock that forces awareness. The shock of being told of imminent death over which there seems to be no control forces a person to develop new perspectives on life. In reaction to the diagnosis Dean Bishop said: "With me it was a tremendous emotional shock.... When there was a date placed on the length of time I had to live, it was almost something I could not stand."

Doug Scott revealed that "I was really shaken up badly. I felt deeply traumatized, scared, fearful, and hopeless."

Bishop, Scott, and Searle were almost paralyzed with fear and shock following their diagnoses. However, their anger and realization that someone else was predicting the outcome of their lives gave impetus to change and growth.

The key words here are "something I could not stand" and "I was really shaken up badly." Growth often follows shock or crisis, and sometimes we even precipitate a crisis as a way of getting things moving, in order to change and grow.

Gregory Bateson believed that his diagnosis was therapeutic because "it stirred me up." His initial reaction to his diagnosis, however, was to go into a neutral state, to pull in his head and let the waves go over him. He did not fight the illness and felt that he accepted death. He did not have any supernatural beliefs about death—in fact, he thought that life after death was not a healthy concept—but rather assumed that death was right and necessary, that "the pretty words written on the blackboard have to be deleted, be reduced to entropy, and form chalk dust. The pattern," he said, "does not survive the interruption." He felt that his acceptance of death was different from the usual reaction, which is to get out and do things. He felt that he was much more a good Taoist than "a good American."

STAGE ONE: AWARENESS

☐ *2. Acceptance* Like Bateson, others finally accepted the diagnosis. Hans Selye understood the scientific reality of his situation: "I completely accepted the diagnosis as terminal, having no reason to doubt it. I accepted the finality and asked myself what was best for me to do during the year I had left to live." He decided to proceed with the writing of his autobiography, *The Stress of My Life*, which was something he thought he could do well. Through his writing he wanted to accomplish as much as he could for the good of humanity.

Doug Scott also accepted and believed the diagnosis that he had cancer; he could not deny what was happening to him. As he looked back and reflected on the time of his diagnosis, he realized that even before he became ill he knew that his life should and possibly could change. One of the strongest messages that emerged from his disease was "change or else."

On a Friday Scott was told that he required surgery; on the following Monday he left for a two-week trip to California. He had decided that he needed time to get himself together, body and soul. He had never been to California and had always wanted to go; now there was a chance he might never do so. He asked his doctor whether two weeks would make any difference to the outcome of his surgery. The doctor felt that the malignancy would not change significantly in that short time and suggested that Scott make the trip. The decision to go to California was part of Scott's choice to live; he chose life rather than hospital dependency. Something inside him said he had to go to California, to get himself feeling strong, built up, and ready.

Acceptance of our mortality is difficult or impossible for most of us. Doug Scott learned "... to accept death in a way that I never had before—in fact, I had essentially denied the inevitability of death." Yet when he came face to face with death, he let go of the death phobia he had carried all his life. He now accepts and recognizes his mortality and his fragility, which have, paradoxically, allowed him to experience and accept life more fully.

Ann Latimer acknowledged that she had had difficulty even thinking about death and that she had always been terrified of the idea. She never did fully accept her diagnosis or the fact of death. Her fear for her life and her rights turned into a fight against disease rather than a self-affirming struggle for life.

Jim Searle found acceptance particularly hard. When his friends suggested that he take a trip around the world or head to the islands to die in the arms of a Tahitian woman, he knew they thought they were talking to a dying man. They helped him, however, because they made him realize that in no way was he ready to die. His main reaction to the diagnosis was to keep outwardly calm by rationalizing his problems rather than by reacting emotionally to them; but inside, Searle felt numb, terrified, detached, and alone.

☐ *3. Struggle* The third element of awareness is the recognition of struggle. Shock forces the realization that there is indeed a balance point. This balance point is the resolution of the struggle between our destructive and life-affirming tendencies.

One side of this struggle, as described by some of the participants, was an awareness of negative influences such as loss, problems, guilt, helplessness, the feeling of being on a dead-end street, of not being able to find a solution, resolve a situation, or find a way out. The other side was an awareness of the desire or will to live. It is a paradox that only the prospect of death brings the beauty of life into sharp, clear focus.

Scott and Latimer describe their awareness of the life-death struggle. As Scott faced the long-term issue of his life, he realized he was still not sure whether his life was worth living: "I just felt as though I was on a scale which teetered and it could go either way. I realized at this point that my process was a life-death struggle." Latimer felt torn between giving up and fighting back: "I think there are two forces that are clashing. There's a part that wants to lie down and give up and a part that wants to go on."

Dean Bishop hated to think that he would never see the beauty of nature again. Through his love of nature—mountains, valleys, trees, and wildlife—he recognized the depth of his attachment to life. As he walked the trails he and his wife had just cut through their ranch, he realized that he might never be witness to spring again, never see the beautiful bloom of the ash tree that marked for him the beginning of a new season. These thoughts induced a lot of crying and considerable questioning, such as "Why me?" It was a long time before he could ask "Why not me?" and start to look at the implications of his disease.

Like Bishop, others found the struggle debilitating but ultimately life-affirming. Doug Scott said:

> I felt helpless, like a victim in the clutch of some relentless kind of force that was gradually going to choke out my life.... I began to get just the beginning of the sense in myself that I was going to fight or something positive was going to happen.

The beginning of awareness occurred for these people when they found themselves in overwhelming crises and felt control of their lives slipping away. Then, consciously or unconsciously, they tipped the scales of the struggle in their own favor. Each attained a measure of awareness sufficient to help extend and improve the quality of his or her life.

If individuals confronted with a terminal diagnosis say, "I knew it; this fits with the pattern or scripting of my life; I knew this would happen to me; nothing works out for me," and so on, then, unwittingly or perhaps willingly, they make their lives dependent on the medical profession. By fulfilling the expectations of medical expertise and the expectations of family, friends, and themselves, they are likely to die at a time close to the predicted date of death.

Author Marilyn Ferguson, publisher of *Brain/Mind Bulletin*, describes the role of altered awareness as the single most important discovery in modern medical science. The more self-aware we become, the healthier and more vibrant we will be. For me, the experience of awareness has been as if a veil was ripped from my eyes—a veil I didn't even know was there. For others, new awareness may occur during meditation, at the sight of breathtaking beauty, or during an unexpected experience, like a revelation. Awareness is an expanded consciousness of self in relation to the world.

☐ 5
STAGE TWO: MEANING

For this is the journey that men and women make; to find themselves. If they fail in this, it doesn't matter much else what they find.
—James A. Michener

As their awareness increased, the participants in my study felt the need to understand the meaning of what seemed to be a hopeless and depressing diagnosis. They faced a fate from which they had been told there was no escape. Some of them acknowledged that at the time they were out of touch with their feelings and with their senses. Imminent death triggered questions concerning their basic values and approach to life: instead of accepting their diagnoses unthinkingly, they searched for meaning in their suffering and were able to make fundamental changes in their attitudes and their lifestyles.

The acceptance of his diagnosis produced deep emotions within Dean Bishop. He questioned his desire to live and his attitude toward living. Until that time he had managed his feelings by denying and repressing them. He now realized the urgency of confronting and resolving emotional conflict.

Bishop's father had been an angry man, and Dean did not get along with him very well. Through his authority and heartless aggression the father had succeeded in diminishing the spark of life in the boy. Dean remembers deciding, at the age of only six years, that he did not want to live. Following this conscious decision, he became very sick and spent the next two years in bed. Later he counterbalanced this death wish by deciding to take charge of his own life and to manipulate his father by being smarter. What he had not realized at the age of six was that he, like his father, had now incorporated anger as a major style or way of living. By making the decision to live his life less aggressively and more compassionately, Dean placed his feet again on the path to health.

Doug Scott also was forced to reconsider parts of his life. As a result of coming face to face with death, he has let go of his fear of it—a fear he had carried all his life. In fact, having essentially denied the inevitability of death until this experience; he now accepts it. He is writing a book, called *Life Over Death*, which deals with elements of his own experience that relate to holistic notions of living and health. He wants to share what has helped him and how he has helped himself.

As soon as he received his diagnosis, Scott was aware of the struggle between the forces of life and death. He recalls not knowing which way the balance would tip: if he had an isolated tumor he had a chance; on the other hand, if it had spread, his life was over. Before surgery, he built himself up to a psychological and physical peak; after the operation, he felt weak and sore and his stomach was in a knot. As he faced the long-term issue of his life, he was still not sure that his life was worth it. He would find himself getting depressed "like a victim in the clutch of some relentless force that was gradually going to choke out his life."

Watching the movie *Death Takes a Holiday* made Scott aware of the inviting part of death, which promises peace and an end to struggle. He began to realize that life is struggle and that this is part of the challenge and excitement of living.

The diagnosis itself proved to be profoundly meaningful to both Bishop and Scott. The shock of imminent death focused their awareness on what they valued in life. It appeared that when an authority (other than themselves) predicted the end of life, a strong drive for survival and rejuvenation emerged. They re-evaluated the meaning of their illness and of their lives, and this turned out to be crucial in helping them to determine their future direction. Meaning became focused on *self* and on *values*. An affirmation of self was very evident for Dean Bishop: "The real function and meaning of the diagnosis was to ask myself, 'What do I want to do with the time I've got left? How do I want to enjoy it? Am I willing to do, live, and enjoy?'"

Values such as beauty, joy, honesty, achievement, humor, and purpose were now etched clearly in their minds and hearts. It was as if a pristine realization of the true essence of life had emerged. Bishop realized that beauty and joy were imperative life-giving values. The following two quotations are his.

☐ *Beauty:* "I have a ranch, and as I walked the trails where there are wild game, deer, quail, squirrels, coons, and clear streams with lots of fish, I would think, 'Well, maybe I won't see this again.'"

☐ *Joy:* "I want to live as long as it's fun, enjoyable, and I have lots of people around me."

☐ *Honesty:* Jim Searle acknowledged that his lack of honesty interfered with his life and allowed cancer to grow. One night when he was jogging, he became aware that his body was actually making his cancer messages accessible, if he would only stop and listen to them. He believed that his cancer of the kidney (he passed blood instead of urine) was from not "pissing" out the truth, but from holding it in. (He had had a sexual relationship with his teenage stepdaughter and had not yet shared this fact with his wife, her mother.) The tumor in his jaw, he felt, was the result of being close-mouthed and not speaking straight out, honestly. He also thought that the cancer in his right wrist was symbolic of his inability to be assertive with his children by not setting and insisting on limits. This left him operating from a position of weakness rather than strength.

Searle's therapist asked him to give reasons for wanting to die. Searle thought he didn't want to die, but at the same time he could also understand why he might see his dying as a kind of punishment.

☐ *Achievement and Creativity:* Bateson acknowledged that "My book *Mind and Nature: A Necessary Unity* owes its existence to cancer." Both Bateson and Selye found that expressing themselves through writing gave them a sense of purpose and fulfillment. Selye shared that he "wanted to accomplish through my writing as much as I could for the

STAGE TWO: MEANING

good of humanity. It would give me an objective in life and it would amuse me."

☐ *Humor:* Humor always played a part in Searle's life, he felt that it helped to keep him alive: "I think I would be dead without humor, especially since the diagnosis." Because he felt this area was too long ignored in psychology texts, he devised and taught a course called the Psychology of Humor.

☐ *Purpose:* Searle said: "I haven't died when others with similar diagnoses did because the purpose or value of the disease made sense to me and it may not have for others who died." He believed that his cancer was giving him the message to be more honest with himself and others.

☐ *Fight:* Hans Selye felt that "the experience of cancer has shown me that one can go on fighting even with something that everyone says will kill you."

Selye was not sure that he understood the full meaning of his cancer, although he knew the experience of having it had a great influence on him. His understanding of life and its meaning came from within himself, from his relationship to his environment and other people. One of his most cherished mottoes was "It is not what happens to you that is important, it is the way you take it." The experience of cancer afforded Selye the opportunity to learn that he was able to fight illness effectively even though he had been told by medical authorities that his particular disease would kill him.

Ann Latimer refused to give in even when her doctors regarded her case as hopeless. Although the disease made her slow down, the diagnosis made her want to live even more. She knew she had to keep on fighting. She would let no one play God with her; she was the one who controlled her body. Ann believed that she had played a part in recovering her health, even for a short time. She felt she had not died when others had because she had not sat back and let death take over. Death was something she had never really considered before, and she guessed she had always been a bit frightened of it.

The need to feel that there is meaning in life is well attested to by psychiatrist and professor Victor Frankl in *Man's Search for Meaning*. In this book he illustrated the connection between meaning and survival by describing the prisoners in the Nazi concentration camps. He observed that those prisoners who saw meaning in life, or who gave it meaning, demonstrated a surprising degree of strength and resistance. Finding this meaning proved to be a decisive factor for survival. Many of those who lacked such incentive gave up and died. Albert Einstein phrased it differently, but just as forcefully, when he suggested that the man who regards his life as meaningless is not merely unhappy but hardly fit to live.

Meaning may be the missing link between mind and illness or between energy (thought process) and matter (the body). David Bohm, an eminent theoretical physicist at the University of London, has said that "meaning which is simultaneously mental and physical can serve as the link or bridge between two realms. This link is indivisible, like two sides of a continuous Möbius strip. Information contained in thought, on the 'mental' side, is at the same time a chemical activity on the 'material' side" (*Brain/Mind Bulletin*, vol. 10, no. 10, 1985).

It is essential to straddle this bridge and to study the language or symptoms of illness, to give voice to whatever is manifesting itself. What is your sore throat, your rash, or the pain in your chest saying to you? The answer is there for you to see and hear,

STAGE TWO: MEANING

and it's there on your behalf. Listen to the message of your symptom.

In *The Voice of Illness* professor of religion Aarne Siirala points out that Freud was one of the first to discover that the symptoms of disease in nervous patients had meanings. It was upon this discovery that the psychoanalytic method of treatment was based.

Gregory Bateson was well prepared to find meaning in his illness. Throughout his life he had been in search of the patterns underlying our theories of ourselves and of an understanding of how these patterns contribute to our ideas of man. Following his diagnosis of cancer, he brought his thinking to bear on the institution of medicine. Bateson felt that medical science should, in all its forms of expression—technical, social, therapeutic—express human nature fully; that our theory of mind-body relations requires a synthesis:

> We operate on the assumption that medicine really knows something; and if medicine knows something, then cancer is a very special disease about which they know nothing. It's all very mysterious and wonderful. The fact of being labeled terminal is again wonderful. But all this presumes that medicine knows something, whereas the truth of it is, they know very little at all. They know a few tricks; in the last thirty years they've developed a stock of tricks.

But as to knowing how the body works, having any sort of solution to the mind-body problem, doctors, to Bateson, seemed to be still in the Middle Ages. He said that "Homeostasis, in 1890, was their last new idea," and he hoped that perhaps by 2050 the medical profession would have aspired to some innovative thinking.

Bateson believed that people get sick by "being fucked up or fucking themselves up" and was willing to believe he had put in his "two bits' worth" toward that. He felt that he could have improved on his personal relationships and wished they had been more fulfilling. He felt that he had been lazy, leaving undone things that he felt he should have finished. He also believed that the world he was living in was "one hell of a mess" and that his public statements were a good deal more optimistic than he really felt. He described the world as a mixture of greed and folly and felt frustrated and depressed by its stupidity.

Bateson was bored by public office. Governor Gerald Brown had appointed him to the Board of Regents of the University of California, but he found it tiring. He felt that boredom was almost a toxic phenomenon, and that it might even create a chemical reaction in one's body. After his diagnostic surgery, he found he was bored by his hospital visitors, all of whom wanted "little bits of Brown, or little bits of Bateson." He felt that there might be a connection between boredom and getting sick and that somehow boredom was related to anger.

For Doug Scott, the relationship between his attitude and his illness was very clear: he felt that he expected to be sick, that being sick fit his life pattern. He realized he had some distinct and severe emotional/psychological problems, that he had strong negative tendencies implanted in him, that his struggle at this stage of his life was a life-or-death one. Scott knows now that the recognition of this dichotomous struggle was another stage of recovery.

Before and during the time of his illness Scott was under considerable stress. He was finishing up his doctoral degree, had just separated from his wife and children, and was living with a woman he had been seeing for two years. He had not handled this stress well and in his reading on self-healing recognized the central importance of stress in degenerative illnesses, particularly cancer.

STAGE TWO: MEANING

Scott thinks he contributed to or participated in his disease by the unsatisfactory way in which he handled his new relationship and is convinced that this was a significant factor in lowering the strength of his immune system. Not knowing how to change or leave it, he stayed in the new relationship long after it had failed. He remembers saying to a therapist, shortly before his first tumor was diagnosed, that he could feel the effect of all the upsets on his system. He was consuming a lot of energy within himself and, in fact, lost fifteen pounds in six months. His system did not have the resources or strength to look after itself the way it needed to, and this fit a lifelong pattern. His pathology included fear, inability to express feelings and needs, self-neglect, and withdrawal.

Scott's body had become a metaphor for his position on the continuum of illness and health. His symptoms became more and more meaningful to him, assisting him along the Healing Path.

☐ 6
STAGE THREE: CHOICE

Man is ultimately self-determining. Man does not simply exist, but always decides what his existence will be, what he will become in the next moment. —Victor Frankl

Increased awareness of our own experience helps underline the importance of the ability to choose for ourselves. Victor Frankl described choice as the last of the human freedoms—as the ability to choose our attitude in any given set of circumstances, to choose our own way. He believed that we *are* ultimately self-determining, that we do not simply exist, but decide what our existence will be, what we will become in the next moment. Rollo May has suggested that it is doubtful whether any of us really begins to live, that is, to affirm and choose our own existence, until we have frankly confronted the terrifying fact that we could wipe out our existence if we chose to do so. Since we are free to die, we are also free to live.

By choice, I mean the selection of an attitude or course of action from among various possibilities. This often means relinquishing familiar ways of being. When your life is teetering at the balance point, you are forced to *choose*. The choice of living or dying was frighteningly clear to the participants in this investigation.

Hans Selye believed that the element of choice between dying and living should be taught to both adults and children, that it is important information for children to learn and grow with, and "that a knowledge of how to live one's life is much more important than all the laws of geometry."

He called his concept of how to live his "code of behavior"; it could just as well be called a philosophy of life. He believed in having and knowing what you want, in going after it, and in not trying to satisfy only society. For example, he said that society's most highly valued or greatest measure of achievement is money; and this was not acceptable to him. The important thing is to know yourself and make your own choices.

Selye affirmed that everything he knew or learned had come from "fighting for my aim." He has been called "a medical Einstein." His concept of an ultimate reality was similar to Albert Einstein's: both believed that God is the laws of nature, that those laws have always existed and will always endure, even when humankind no longer exists. Selye described his research findings as "nature's answers to his questions." He believed that if you ask the right question, nature will always answer you correctly. "Nature," he said, "never makes a mistake." His scientific research was primarily concerned with

STAGE THREE: CHOICE

formulating the right questions and using his powers of observation to see what others did not see.

Selye was born in Austria during the reign of Emperor Franz Josef. He was taught by Benedictine fathers in a little town called Komárom halfway between Budapest and Vienna. Selye was a stubborn sort of person, very much a fighter. At the age of ten he was a fat and flabby child and, much to his unhappiness, the boys in his school amused themselves by frequently beating him up. Consequently, he transformed his room into a gymnasium with parallel bars and rings, trained hard, and then went out and "beat up everybody." He developed his muscles to prevent others from attacking and causing him shame and humiliation. Selye feels that this childhood experience increased his self-confidence and that his strength of mind followed. He took great satisfaction in the fact that he could "beat up all the tough guys" if and when he chose. He believed that how you feel about your body can affect how you feel about yourself.

He felt that it is important, whether you have a splitting headache, a toothache, a bellyache, or any other ailment, to acknowledge that you have some control over what is happening.

Selye learned a lesson from his father that proved to be one of his strongest motivations. The father knew that the boy liked to ride and to cheer him up during the devastation of the First World War bought him a full-blooded Arabian pony. It had the peculiar habit of bucking, not by kicking up either its front feet or back feet but by jumping up with all four feet in the air at the same time and making a sound like "Kweeech." Kweechka, as the horse came to be called, threw Selye all the time. When it would "Kweeech," Selye wound up on the ground. Three times he broke his arm, and each time this happened, his father, who was a doctor, would take him up to surgery and put his arm in a cast. He would tell Selye he must remount Kweechka right away, because if he let himself be beaten once, he would always be afraid and would never ride again. His father believed that this philosophy held true not only regarding horses but also concerning every challenge in life. Selye adopted this concept.

Although the awareness that he was going to die was extremely unpleasant, Selye also realized that he had the choice of a variety of reactions. He chose not to allow treatment with chemotherapy under any circumstances. He knew all too well that chemotherapy could do irreparable damage to his healthy blood cells. "I would not and will not take chemotherapy under any circumstances." Dean Bishop expressed the same need to be able to choose: "I know, without question, that if I become extremely depressed I could die anytime I want. When I choose to die, I'll be able to go rather quickly."

Bishop felt strongly that he was the captain of his ship, that he determined whether the voyage would be successful or disastrous. There was no doubt in his mind that he made his own decision to live or die.

Jim Searle discovered his desire to live in an interesting way. When he first had his nephrectomy (surgical removal of a kidney)—before his terminal diagnosis—he asked the surgeon what his recovery odds were. The reply was something like 60/40, and Searle said to himself, "Those aren't my odds!" He was not going to let someone else determine the probability of his life's outcome.

Searle chose to run, study Tai Chi, investigate and use vitamin C, and become involved in psychotherapy. "I decided to choose my own alternative methods of treatment to get more in touch with myself."

Searle rejected four different forms of medical treatment: (1) surgery, because the doctor could not keep going back into his lung; (2) radiation, because it would burn his lungs faster than it would the cancer; (3) chemotherapy, because it was difficult to treat renal cell cancer with drugs, and (4) treatment with a female hormone, the side effects of which would be the loss of sexual potency and possible breast development. Searle talked to the man who had developed the female hormone procedure; he did not recommend it for Searle because he had only one spot on his lung. He cautioned Searle that things sometimes get worse with hormones because they apparently interfere with the immune system.

Ann Latimer had always insisted on her own point of view. At the age of a year and a half she had declared that since she had a right shoe and a left shoe, she must therefore have a right sock and a left sock. Early in her struggle with cancer she felt her will opposing that of the doctors.

The medical profession's lack of sensitivity was evident in the radiation clinic. Latimer resented the side effects of her radiation, some of which she felt were the result of inaccurate focusing of the X rays. She was surprised that the clinics did not give out booklets informing people of possible radiation effects. She was dismayed by the lack of respect for privacy and dignity; for example, in her presence a doctor told another woman that since he had done surgery and radiation, there was nothing more he could do for her and that he might just as well make her comfortable for what remained of her life. The arrogance of doctors infuriated Latimer.

Latimer also resented being put on a teaching ward for observation by first-year residents, interns, and students without her foreknowledge or consent; she was not allowed to make her own choice in the matter.

She suggested that others not let their doctors "play God" with them. She supported the individual's right to make some decisions, saying that each person owns his or her body. Latimer felt that listening to one's doctor is important, but that listening to oneself is equally important. She believed that if doctors want a patient's respect, they must also respect the patient. Her advice to those dissatisfied with their doctors was to get another one, and another, until satisfied. One of her doctors, whom she liked, said that she had made a liar out of all of them, having been "at death's door" and not died. He said she had proved that doctors are not always right. He was the only doctor she knew who admitted this—or anything like it. In spite of extreme dissatisfaction with her medical treatment, Latimer was still able to appreciate the help her doctors gave her.

    This brings to light an interesting parable. The participants accepted the scientific evidence of a terminal diagnosis: what they did not accept was the implied message that there was nothing they could do. Each became his or her personal agent for change, action, and continuing life. Each of them *chose* to actively change.

7
STAGE FOUR: WILL

Where there's a will, there's a way.

Will is the fulcrum of the Healing Path, the crossroads that lead to health on the one hand or hopelessness and death on the other.

Will is the stage at which your thinking must be translated into positive action. If this does not happen, there is a tendency toward dependency, which can lead to apathy, hopelessness, despair and death.

Roberto Assagioli, a psychiatrist and pioneer of modern psychology, has described will as "the function in closest relation to the self, the most direct expression of the self." He says it can be experienced as "an intelligent energy directed toward a definite aim, having a purpose." The crisis of the diagnosis and the ensuing life-death struggle put the six participants in my investigation in touch with an inner energy or power that gave them the experience of "willing." In *Act of Will*, Assagioli says:

> The discovery of the will in oneself, and even more the realization that the self and the will are intimately connected, may come as a real revelation which can change, often radically, a man's self-awareness and his whole attitude toward himself, other people, and the world. He perceives that he is a living subject endowed with the power to choose, to relate, to bring about changes in his own personality, in others, in circumstances. This enhanced awareness, this "awakening" and vision of new, unlimited potentialities for inner expansion and outer action, gives a new feeling of confidence, security, joy—a sense of "wholeness."

That wholeness can be the beginning of a sense of the power in belief, action, and healing.

Informing the participants of the terminal nature of their disease played a part in the development of their will to live. The challenge of death inspired the motivation to live.

Dean Bishop's will to live developed after he realized that he might not have the chance to make any choice. His sense of challenge and identity had always come primarily from his work. The diagnosis was a definite and major turning point, forcing him to examine the meaning of his life. Following this examination, he asked himself: "What do I really want out of life? What do I want to do with the time I've got left? Am I *willing* to live and enjoy life?"

He had not been aware of the power of his will to live. "I wasn't sure I had much will to live. That developed after I realized I might not have the chance." He needed the shake-up of a terminal diagnosis to awaken him to what was really important in his life—to realize that he himself was influencing his living and dying.

Hearing that her life was coming to an end helped Ann Latimer realize how much she treasured life and wanted to go on. "The diagnosis made me *want* to live more." Motivation played a distinct role.

Hans Selye believed that the concept of not having a future was a reason that people died of so-called incurable illnesses. He had been physically active within the limitations of his age, but when he was in his early fifties, osteoarthritis forced him to undergo two major operations to replace both his hip joints with artificial ones. Although he was limited in the sports in which he could participate (his hip joints resided in a bottle on his office shelf), he swam and exercised regularly and often rode his bicycle to work, weather permitting. A typical day would start with a television performance in the morning, a radio show in the afternoon, an evening plane to New York to deliver a lecture, and a return flight to Montreal the next morning. Once, having just returned from France, he took off again for Tokyo, Kyoto, Sayama, Taiwan, and back—all in fourteen days.

Selye always had a strong motivational drive, and following the diagnosis of a malignant tumor in his thigh he discovered he had as much or more motivation than usual. Believing that he had a definite purpose in life, he did not feel like a man whom everyone pities because he is going to die. He went ahead with ten-to-twenty year plans for his institute, feeling that if somebody else was going to be in charge, the institute would still be carrying on his work.

In 1978 the Sloan-Kettering Institute, the largest cancer institute in the world, held a symposium on cancer and death at Selye's International Institute of Stress. It was by invitation only and was composed of ten Canadians and ten Americans. The results are published in *Cancer, Stress and Death*, edited by

Professor Stacey Day of the Sloan-Kettering Institute. Out of this gathering came agreement on the possibility of tumor regression resulting from motivation. In the years following the symposium, Selye had his library staff compile a major collection of information related to motivation.

Selye was also motivated by what the French call *la joie de vivre* (the joy of living)—or what he called the "will to live." This force can help a person strike out against any kind of disease, including minor ones.

Selye proved his belief in the paramount importance of the will to live by recovering completely. As he said:

> I believe that if a person gives up the will to live then that person is dead with no chance of survival.

Doug Scott remembers mobilizing his will through determination and action:

> I can recall the instant when I said to myself, yes, I do want to live, I am going to recover, I'm going to start exercising and get myself strong, rehabilitate, and go on with my life. I was then very much aware of the life-death pull.... I know that I turned around my psychological/emotional state as I went from feeling helpless, doomed, victimized, despondent, and weak to feeling very strong, confident and determined that I was going to come through. I resolved to continue healing and to repair my life.... I developed a strong conviction that this would be my intention and that's what did happen.

Scott recognized that he was a major source of stress to himself; he now feels that he was getting strong messages from his own system, especially at the time of his diagnosis, warning him of the need to change. Until he became ill, he had been afraid to make changes, afraid to risk, unwilling to change

STAGE FOUR: WILL

and grow. He now believes that illness may be the result of a refusal to change.

As he looks back, he realizes that the point when he expressed the wish that his luck would change was a significant turning point. He can see a clear pattern from that moment on: it was not that his "luck" was changing but that *he* was starting to change from a passive attitude of hoping that something or someone would change him to a realization and acceptance that only he could do something to make the change. He was questioning his self-worth, the purpose of his life, and his own sense of strength and power. It was then that he started to mobilize himself and his resources.

Will is the fulcrum of the Healing Path. The first three stages—awareness, meaning, and choice—are essentially psychological. The latter three stages—responsibility, strategies, and change—are more social, more related to environment. *Will is action.* Awareness of the will to live must be transformed into active responsibility for change.

☐ 8
STAGE FIVE: RESPONSIBILITY

Are we to assume there are no hazards in inaction and purposelessness? Does the body pay no price for emotional, mental, and physical lethargy and stupefaction?
—Norman Cousins

The will to live demands the acceptance of responsibility for one's own destiny, for making basic choices oneself.

Doug Scott's awareness of the life and death struggle produced the sense that he was going to fight or that something positive was going to happen.

He went to Los Angeles, California, discovered the Center for the Healing Arts, the Simonton tapes on relaxation and healing, and some outstanding articles on self-healing. Scott knows that he turned around his psychological/emotional state with the help of these resources. He expected that his surgery would be successful and that he would be able to continue healing himself and repair his life. He developed a strong conviction that this would happen and, in fact, that *is* what has happened.

The meaning that cancer had for Scott is somewhat paradoxical. He learned that although he has a fragile, sensitive system, he can still be strong and resourceful. His acceptance of his mortality and fragility has allowed him to accept and experience life more fully.

Being responsible means making the choice or decision to transform intellectual willingness into life-affirming action. As the participants in this study became increasingly aware of their involvement in their illness, they were able to assume more responsibility for themselves. They realized that they could actively participate in becoming healthy. The acceptance of this responsibility transformed their will into responsible action.

This was not an easy transition for these people to make. It took less effort to feel self-pity concerning their condition, to indulge in feelings of guilt for having let themselves get sick, and to simply blame the world for their misfortune. It took time, thought, and creative energy for these individuals to learn to accept this responsibility wholly.

As Dean Bishop said, "It was a long time before I could change from asking 'Why me?' to 'Why not me?' I *had* to deal with the deep emotions this question touched in me."

Gregory Bateson felt strongly that taking individual responsibility for illness—as a recipient of the message of illness and as a respondent to that message—is central to healing. His view of his own experience of illness as a placebo was one that he created and invested in. He chose to experience his illness as an adventure and assumed responsibility for opening himself to the experience and accepting the consequences. He felt that by believing it to be a positive changing experience, it became so.

Bateson accepted responsibility for the unconventional stance he took—created with his mind—toward his healing. He thought, however, that usually the patient is more receptive to the conventional messages transmitted by doctors and that, to the extent that the medical profession has educated people to receive *its* messages and to relinquish their responsibility to it, it is responsible for the structure the patient places on his or her experience. "We live the myths in which our lives are embedded. The myths acquire that credibility. It is to these myths that the medical profession... owes responsibility."

Bateson stated that nothing outward is different from what is inward. He did not believe in that distinction or separation. His argument was that they are the same thing—thus the "grave responsibility of doctors in all parts of their practice."

He believed that medical people acknowledge only the brain, that the mind does not exist for them. For him there was nothing supernatural about the mind and it did not exist outside the body—except insofar as one's perception is part of it and one uses one's fingers to count with. "And," he said, "that would take your mind as far as the outer galaxies of Pluto, if you happen to be an astronomer."

Bateson stated that the "Cartesian split between mind and body is nonsense. The basis of that union is that the mind runs on difference, and difference is not a visible characteristic. The difference between the table and the pepperpot is not physics. But even though we get these two together," he continued, "we still haven't included in that picture the problem of aesthetics and beauty, and we really don't know how that belongs. Without this being linked in, we're in a pretty arid condition. One has to accept on faith that one can sooner or later link these in somehow. But," he said, "I don't know how to do it."

As responsibility for self developed, the participants were gradually able to explore the idea that perhaps they had played a part in becoming sick. As noted earlier, Doug Scott realized that, "In terms of feeling responsible for participating, I think the major factor was the unsatisfactory way in which I handled my relationship. Initially I unconsciously contributed to my disease by not recognizing that what I was doing was stressful.... When I got sick I wasn't aware that I was out of touch with my feelings."

Dean Bishop felt that being out of touch with his feelings contributed substantially to his illness. Since his brush with death, he has become a man who loves people and is not afraid to reach out and experience joy in conversation with them. He, too, realizes now that he was out of touch with his feelings and that in some way this contributed to his illness.

Bishop had two close friends who also had multiple myeloma and who died less than two years after their diagnoses—the outcome that had been predicted for him. One of these individuals was a scientist who, when his services were no longer needed, lost all desire to live. Bishop feels that it was sadness and loss of meaning, purpose, and desire to live that contributed to his friend's death.

Dean Bishop regained control of his life. "What is important is my ability to program my own life and to fulfill those things I want to do rather than put them off."

Although Jim Searle could not bear to be alone when he first heard the diagnosis, he also realized that he had to take time for himself. He felt afraid and vulnerable. He became aware that, all his life,

STAGE FIVE: RESPONSIBILITY

he'd been living with groups of people—at college, in the army, with a wife and family. He overcame his fear of loneliness by taking summer retreats and found that he was relaxed and happy during these times. He looked for a place of solitude and found it first in meditation and then in real life. He rented a room by the ocean and there he practiced Tai Chi and yoga, listened to the tides, and watched the moon.

He felt that he influenced the course of his illness in a number of different ways. He talked to Linus Pauling, author and international expert on vitamin C, and decided to take the vitamin regularly; he also visited a metabolic therapist, attended healing workshops, and kept a personal journal. In addition, he took Laetrile, a cyanide-containing compound extracted from peach stones, which has been used in the treatment of various forms of cancer despite a lack of scientific evidence of its value.

As Searle put it: "I knew it was up to me to change things now—to maintain some kind of control over treatment, to keep exploring and investigating, to be critical of all treatments, alternative and traditional, and to hold onto a sense of humor."

As these people realized that medical science was not going to provide a cure, there began a transition from dependency on doctors and other authorities to a discovery of their own autonomy and fulfillment. By assuming responsibility for their disease, they were able to use their illness as an opportunity for change. There was a growing realization for them all that disease is composed of far more than just the physical. How to move toward change and transition became their next task.

9

STAGE SIX: STRATEGIES

The truth in the world of man is not to be found as the content of knowledge, but only as human existence. One does not reflect upon it, one does not express it, one does not perceive it, but one lives it and receives it as life.—Martin Buber

The strategies of the participants for improving their health and their quality of life were similar and yet diverse enough to meet their individual needs, interests, and purposes. They all felt that, in some way or other, they had influenced the course of their disease and health. Their strategies included exercise, psychotherapy, belief in the immune system, visualization, creativity, fighting back or fighting for life space, spiritual participation, and humor. The belief in self, that *they* were their own greatest resource for healing, resonates throughout these strategies.

☐ EXERCISE

Doug Scott always liked physical activity—running, exercise, and working out in a gym. While in hospital, he would exercise by going up and down the eight flights of stairs, two at a time, five times a day.

Jim Searle loved to run. He read about the beneficial effects of running and how it could help to increase one's white blood-cell count, or leucocytes. White blood cells produce antibodies and help to protect the body against foreign invaders. Running became one of the most important influences on his desire to live and helped him to feel completely alive and much more aware of his body.

> I decided that running was important for me. I began to read about the beneficial effects of running on strengthening the immune system. I found it calmed me down and helped me deal with stress. Running has been one of the very powerful experiences influencing my desire to live. When I am running, I feel alive and completely aware of my body, as if I am fully occupying my body. Running is like a return to myself, my body, having been living in my head for years.

The exaltation and excitement of running the 1977 marathon in Honolulu was one of the peak experiences of his life. Before dawn, three thousand runners took off like an immense ameba, spreading out over the hills near Waikiki Beach. Because there

STAGE SIX: STRATEGIES

were so many people on the road that nobody could hear the starter gun, a synchronized military cannon sent them off. Searle loved all those people. They felt crazily happy together and applauded each other as they left the starting line. During the race the participants ran and walked, but Searle and two other runners decided that they had to run across the finish line as a symbolic gesture of their attitude toward the race of life. When they finished, they were grimy and sweaty, but they were embraced by Hawaiians and decorated with leis.

☐ PSYCHOTHERAPY

Dean Bishop was extremely relieved to find a therapist he could trust and to whom he could unburden himself about the confusion and anxiety that he had been carrying for years. He said, "Being able to get into therapy has tremendously relieved my stress. I think this is the way I've been able to exist. I'm glad I've recognized my feelings of anger and worked them through. Feelings of loss and fatigue have changed through therapy."

Doug Scott has been through quite an extended and intense program of personal psychotherapy. He had a number of therapists, some conventional and some not so. He has engaged in rational emotive therapy, bioenergetics, primal therapy, regressive therapy, and some transactional analysis group therapy. He has explored deeply his relationships with both his parents—his feelings about them and about himself—and learned how the development or nondevelopment of these relationships profoundly affected his personal growth. During his regressive therapy, Scott gained a clear sense of himself as a child who was afraid to venture out; to some extent, he is still this way, in his adult life.

Ann Latimer finally accepted her need for help and began seeing a therapist. She realized that she needed people to encourage her and that she felt better when she had more support from others. Hers was a hard-fought battle; she staved off death but used her energy and spirit in a negative manner, which appeared to defy death rather than accept it as part of life.

☐ IMMUNE SYSTEM

Bishop trusts in his own immune system. He also trusts his physical, psychological, and spiritual growth through his psychotherapy with Stephanie Mathews-Simonton and is grateful for the influence of his wife and children who decided to take part in psychotherapy before he did.

> The primary method of fighting my disease was to believe in the possibility that my immune system was healthy and was overcoming the cancer; that it was able to recognize the cancer cells and to actually kill them. This has to be going on because my physical examinations show a high red count and a high white count, which is not common. This is definite evidence that my system is fighting the disease and overcoming it.

He was encouraged by the fact that his thoughts, beliefs, and visualization exercises were having a seemingly direct effect on his illness.

STAGE SIX: STRATEGIES

☐ VISUALIZATION

I used the picture of my X ray for my imagery. I was able to see where the tumor was located, how it looked, and could then visualize the white cells surrounding the tumor, containing it and tearing into it. The aggressive image that I used was white Doberman pinschers surrounding the tumor and tearing it with their teeth.

Although he considers himself an agnostic, Doug Scott did pray a bit to God to spare his life and to help him. In one of his visualizations he saw a figure by the side of the path, a very old man in flowing robes with long white hair and beard, who he feels was a God- or Christ-figure. When Scott approached him, this figure put his arms around him, held him, and comforted him.

When visualizing after surgery, Scott saw within himself a glowing white light, which he recognized as a symbol of health and energy. Scott feels that he did not die when others with a similar diagnosis did because he was more sure that he did not want to die. The extent to which Scott influenced his health will never be known accurately, but he knows that his attitude and feelings changed and that his sense of will and prowess increased. He accounts for what happened by saying that part of it was his own determination to fight in whatever way possible and that another part was hope.

Scott feels that he has influenced his recovery. For example, while in hospital he visualized faithfully. Just before surgery, he recalls having felt completely open to his system and at a deep level of contact with himself. His defenses and armor were gone and he felt he was right into his center. Following the surgery, the pathologist told Scott that there was a very healthy tissue reaction surrounding the tumor and containing it aggressively. Scott attributes the condition of this tissue to his consistent visualizing.

After surgery he combined the surveillance theory with visualization. He visualized white German shepherd dogs patrolling his circulatory system, looking into his canals of blood and snatching out and tearing up any impurities they saw. Visualization bolstered his system and internal resources, and ever since his surgery, he has had no malignancy.

☐ CREATIVITY

Hans Selye felt that the challenge of writing *The Stress of My Life* would motivate him to become well. The act of being creative would draw on and encourage the positive resources within himself.

"That's *Mind and Nature* finished. There's nothing about cancer in it, but the book owes its existence to cancer." The startling theme of this major creative life work by Gregory Bateson is that biological evolution is a *mental* process.

☐ FIGHTING BACK AND FIGHTING FOR

Ann Latimer said, "I haven't died because I've fought. There are two ways of fighting: one is to fight the disease, which I have done, and the other is more like fighting for living space—it's different."

As Doug Scott's understanding of himself and his illness increased, he gained personal power. "My

STAGE SIX: STRATEGIES

determination to fight was growing, as was my desire to do what I could to either heal myself and recover, or to face whatever I had to face with courage and with the support and understanding of those who were close to me."

Gregory Bateson, too, fought in his own way by refusing to submit to chemotherapy or radiation, and he did not take any pain-killing drugs. He wanted his mind to be clear so that he could finish his last book.

☐ *MEDITATION*

Several of the participants found meditation a help, a seeming blend of inner and outer energies.

Doug Scott was told by the medical director of the Los Angeles Center for the Healing Arts that meditation was the royal road to healing. She believes that with this process you can reach the deep structures of consciousness and unconsciousness. "You can," she stated, "even get in touch with the death wish you may have taken on for yourself, and by being aware of it, let go of it."

In hospital, Scott had several profoundly important meditation experiences. The first night, he could see the image of his mother's face and he could feel struggle going on: this message was expressed without words, in a primal kind of scene. The second night, he had a dialogue with her image and said he was giving back the death wishes/death messages she had given him. She replied, "No, you don't know what you are doing. You can't look after yourself." Scott told her that they were her wishes, not his; that he was giving them back to her and she was to take them. She resisted for a while and then agreed. The next night he had a dialogue with the image of

Carl Jung, asking him for advice on how to look after himself. Jung replied that Scott should listen to his own internal wisdom. Another time he randomly opened a book by Jung—right at the page where Jung talks about helping people get in touch with their inner resources!

Following his diagnosis Gregory Bateson spent more time in meditation. He believed that his early-morning, two- to three-hour creative meditations may have helped him recover from cancer. A friend, Rosita, who was an initiate of the Filipino psychic school of surgery and also a healer, confirmed that he was on the mend. Shortly after the operation she examined Bateson and informed him affectionately that he was a fake. She meant that, at present, he did not have a degenerative condition within his chest, that what the doctors had found was a dying cancer. "They were," she said with a grin, "too late!" In fact, during the diagnostic surgery, Bateson's doctors had found quite a bit of dead tissue.

☐ DREAMS

Dean Bishop found dreams particularly helpful. "I use meditation, dreams, memories, and reflections to get in touch with conscious or unconscious events which caused stress and depression in my life and which interfere with the quality of my life."

Bishop has learned about himself through his dreams. When he listens to his dreams and analyzes them, he finds that they tell him what he really thinks about the many persons inside himself. For more than twenty-five years, he had a recurring nightmare in which he dreamed that he was tied down and could only save his life if he could move just one finger. He would struggle and struggle but remain unable to move: when he awakened he would find himself covered in sweat and full of fear. His therapist suggested that, during a meditation, he ask for an explanation of this nightmare. A short time later he had an extremely meaningful dream about two children playing and having fun together. Bishop realized that one child represented his unconscious and the other, his conscious mind. As the children were leaving each other, the child who represented his unconscious told the other child that he would not have to tie him down again, because this child, his conscious mind, was now willing to listen. Bishop felt that this dream explained the tied-down nightmare. The dream has not recurred.

☐ SPIRITUAL NOURISHMENT

Most of the participants said that after the diagnosis they realized that they had somehow lost touch with a higher power, a sense of something larger than themselves. They had become so focused on such goals as prestige or financial success that they had developed a kind of tunnel vision and had quite lost the ability to be in touch with the wisdom of nature, a larger energy, or God.

Dean Bishop definitely believes in life after death and that what lies ahead will be much better. Although he has worked with his therapist and his own internal guide to try to get in touch with the hereafter, he has been able to get only faint glimmers of what it may be like.

He shared his idea of the universal unconscious. "I don't believe in an outside force in a religious sense. I believe in the Jungian concept; that the universal unconscious as a being, or knowledge, is present, and that it comes from some source and goes with you to somewhere." This concept is vague but very meaningful to him.

Doug Scott now has a much stronger sense of there being some kind of force in the universe and feels this life force or life energy connected with him, with the infinite, or the beyond.

Ann Latimer had a faith or trust in something more than herself. She believed that God was there, looking after her and protecting her, otherwise she would not have survived. She prayed to God every night to help her and prayed every morning that she would be fit and well and able to start doing things again.

Aesthetics and the beauty of nature were also sources of spiritual nourishment. Gregory Bateson talked of the importance of the arts in his healing: "The side of life which includes poetry as well as painting and music is fairly important. Certain poetry is really important to me.... I have written two or three poems since the diagnosis. I have moved more toward the arts than away from them since my diagnosis."

Dean Bishop realized the nurturing qualities of nature: "I feel a relationship with the wisdom of nature."

Doug Scott identified with a powerful and life-giving image: "I developed an image which was a symbol for me of the beauty of life and how precious it is: I would rise early to see the sun rising with beautiful color and cloud formations. When I attended a health and healing workshop, I drew a representation of myself as a huge, prominent, smiling sun with waves of energy coming out of me."

☐ HUMOR

Hans Selye experienced the importance of humor: "I love humor and it plays a strong role in my life. I think humor has a creative value, that a good belly laugh helps an awful lot."

Hans Selye's friend Norman Cousins, the editor and writer, had had a connective tissue disease that his doctors had been unable to diagnose accurately but that they thought would be ultimately fatal. In an article published in *The New England Journal of Medicine*, Cousins asserted that it was Selye's concepts that led him to try to cure himself by behavioristic means. One of Cousins's recuperative methods was to watch humorous movies, to make himself laugh more.

Selye was very close to Cousins, whom he called "the laughing man who can tell the funniest jokes," and agreed with his friend that humor had a curative value and that laughter helps to relieve stress immensely. He liked to talk with people who appreciated humor.

Humor had always played a vital part in Jim Searle's life. He said that without it he would certainly be dead—especially since the diagnosis. He kidded his physicians to their faces and spoke humorously about them to others. He even joked about his own fears and dread. He enjoyed teaching and public speaking and had an intuitive feel for an audience. Responding to his listeners' excitement, he could tell whether or not they were with him and, if not, change his style to recapture their attention.

Humor has played an important role for Dean Bishop. It has helped him to lighten issues that otherwise might have dragged him down. He loves fun and interesting conversation and is now emphatically assertive about wanting to live as long as life is fun, enjoyable, and there are lots of people around him. He would not want to live without joy and he has had to work through his fear of dying since his diagnosis. He is not the type to hang on for fear of something beyond.

Humor helped Gregory Bateson increasingly throughout his life, and he suggested that humor might help others move toward health. He felt that the story of his recovery was an amusing joke on the doctors, because they had not expected him to recover.

Ann Latimer agreed: "Humor has helped increasingly throughout my life. Any suggestions for helping others would have something to do with humor."

Doug Scott has always had a good sense of humor but had often held it back. After the diagnosis he found and read articles that helped him see how humor could bolster your health. He has now recognized how important humor is and he is having fun, joking, and enjoying his children and friends.

Scott is an example of one who combined strategies as he journeyed to health. He visualized three times a day, ran daily for three or four miles, ate well, looked after himself more wisely, and put himself first.

The above strategies proved effective in helping these people reveal their beliefs, affirmation of, and joy in living. The strategies became the means whereby they were able to give expression to meaning, purpose, values, and aspirations: the strategies revealed their will to live.

10

STAGE SEVEN: CHANGE

The most important single message I got from my disease was change or else!—Doug Scott

Change is the last stage on the Healing Path and one that continues to evolve as its travellers move toward health. Change is the culmination of the spiral dance of the other stages, each one affecting the other stages and together leading toward change.

The most outstanding change was one of lifestyle. The emphasis for some had been on filling time, and it was now on the quality of that time.

Dean Bishop's life had been geared totally to business endeavors and making money. After the diagnosis of cancer, it was a revelation for him that he was able to make such dramatic and significant changes in his values and ultimately restructure his life. "The change in the direction of my life has brought more joy—in flying, the sunsets, and the beauty of the mountains." When he realized that he could plan a life for himself that included pleasure, his attitude changed from one of despair and depression to one of hope and conviction. He improved his relationships with his family and friends and strengthened his belief in his immune system. He owes his life to his desire to live and to changing his attitudes and lifestyle.

Jim Searle was not religious in the accepted sense. He was brought up as a Jew and did not have a sense of damnation, heaven, or a life hereafter. As a child, he had been taught that, after death, persons are remembered by the deeds they did in life; they continue to live in memory, not on some astroplane. Searle became concerned with living in the present: he felt that this was the only life that he and everyone else have; that death is the end of life. He had difficulty relating to any philosophy that suggested otherwise.

He felt that there is wisdom to be found in nature, but he had no sense of a supernatural being. He thought it possible that we all might be somehow connected to one another by means of some form of energy field. Sometimes he perceived his own energy, or that of another person, in terms of light. He could sense a focusing of energy within himself during his meditations.

Three people who had significantly influenced his life were an English teacher who encouraged his love of public speaking and psychologists Carl Rogers and Fritz Perls.

Before his illness was diagnosed, Searle did not have many close friends, although he knew many people professionally. He suddenly realized his need for others when he was taking the terrifying diagnostic tests and began to put some effort into making a few close friends. When running in the Hawaiian marathon he felt the support of his friend Karl, who stopped and massaged a cramped muscle in Searle's leg during each of the last three or four miles.

Searle had always found it difficult to maintain honesty in his personal relationships. Toward the end of his life he appeared to understand the connection between his own psychological difficulties and the places where his cancer grew. For him, running provided a metaphor: it seems he ran so fast and in so many directions that he never took sufficient time to explore his feelings and confront himself and his mortality.

Relationships with other people changed significantly for Ann Latimer. "Since the diagnosis I've got close to some people.... I've learned that I need people to encourage me. Now, I feel, is the time to ask for help. The more support I can get the better." Unfortunately, she came to this understanding only months before her death. She had become so enmeshed in a system, primarily male, that spends more time, energy, and money on disease care rather than health care that she lost her direction on the Healing Path and spent her energy fighting the system rather than fighting for herself.

Dean Bishop, on the other hand, found the power of the personal connection in time for this interpersonal energy to have an effect on his healing. "Now I have no problem in having close relationships with people.... I enjoy love and touching. I love to have good friends, fellowship, and shared feelings."

Doug Scott's relationships with others changed after his diagnosis. He now feels more freedom to express sadness, anger, fear, and joy, and finds he is much more even-tempered. He is gradually enjoying people more and is better able to give to them and receive from them. "My appreciation of life is much deeper and more finely tuned.... I don't feel warring forces now but feel pretty integrated in terms of conscious and unconscious life space." The change for Scott from self-negation to self-acceptance included an acceptance of mortality.

He became acutely aware of the concept of choice and the nature of purpose when confronted with his diagnosis. He asked himself whether he wanted to go on—was he of use to himself or anyone else? He developed a much stronger sense of some kind of force in the universe and feels that this life force or life energy is connected with him. He now feels a link with the infinite or the beyond. Too many things happened, he feels—such as going to California and unexpectedly meeting people who gave him helpful ideas—that can be explained as mere coincidence. People and new ideas seemed to converge in unpredictable and fortuitous ways and places.

Scott's changes in attitude and lifestyle have affected his health in many ways. Previously, he felt alienated from life. Now he has learned to enjoy life day by day, to live more fully, and not postpone living. He has more energy, his mind and body are clearer, he feels more centered in his life and more definite about what he wants and does not want to do. His personal channels are more direct: his life, activities, and relationships are now a source of pleasure and satisfaction. Since his healing, he has had some dreams of struggle, imagining and fearing the blackness of cancer returning. These dreams serve as reminders to continue monitoring his health and to keep doing positive things for himself.

Scott suggests that in illness you should take heart in every sense of the word: hang on, be strong, take control of yourself, your life, and your situation. He recommends that you find out what you can do for yourself and start doing it. It is important, he feels, to recognize that you are your own greatest resource and to find ways that you can use available outside resources, including physicians, medicine, therapy, visualization, imagery, exercise, nutrition, love, and companionship. He advises you to look after yourself in a whole way, not give up, and take the time to look inward and find your own center of strength.

Scott describes his life now as successful, happy, and rewarding. His illness and recovery have been the culmination of many things he has worked on in therapy: looking back, he perceives his therapy as a preparation for the experience of a terminal diagnosis. He has been able to draw on his therapeutic insights and achieve a more complete understanding of his emotional structure; he has learned how to become his own therapist and counselor and can now do most of this important work on his own.

Gratitude for life, and an awareness of living fully and completely in the present is strikingly evident in the six participants. Dean Bishop discovered that "being myself, finding myself, is my main purpose, to keep looking at better ways of being and hearing myself." He was finally able to stop living to gratify what he assumed were the expectations of others. He was able to look inside himself for his personal truth and then share this freely with whom he chose.

He stated: "I want to take my own direction with more quality. I've made a pledge to myself to not let people lay things on me that I don't like or want. I've resolved to look after myself in real ways."

The most profound change is represented by the fact the these six people lived so long beyond their predicted date of death, changing a death sentence to life. Two of these people are still alive, leading full, productive lives, without any sign of cancer.

11
EXAMINING THE HEALING PATH

Men go abroad to wonder at the height of mountains, at the huge waves of the sea, at the long courses of rivers, at the vast compass of the ocean, at the circular motion of the stars; and they pass by themselves without wondering.—Saint Augustine

This chapter examines the personal experiences of some of my clients and the psychological factors involved in their illness and recovery. I have been very involved with my clients, as they have been with me. I care for them deeply. They came for therapy because they realized that something somewhere in their lives—and, as we found out, in their bodies—was not quite right. Somehow they had lost their balance. Each is unique, but all had the desire to change: to live a lifestyle that allowed for true self-expression.

I will not say that these people have "conquered" illness or cured themselves. I do not believe in that concept. I do believe that they are in the process of healing their lives and in so doing have healed themselves of specific illnesses. It is, however, at this point that the real work begins. Living in health is a dynamic lifelong process. If self-care is neglected because the symptoms of ill health have disappeared, beware. There is a strong probability that the same or related symptoms will reappear.

The first four clients I describe were diagnosed with cancer. The others had different kinds of illnesses. For each of them illness acted as a voice or catalyst, demanding their attention, insisting on change, and ultimately helping them achieve health. All names are pseudonyms.

☐ KIMI OZAWA

Kimi Ozawa, a shy, diminutive woman in her mid-fifties, had a mysterious and beautiful smile. She had just taken early retirement from the United Church as a deaconess when she received the news that her particular form of cancer was terminal. About four and a half years earlier, she had had a radical mastectomy and during the following years had been symptom-free. She returned for medical help in January 1983, when she found swelling lumps between her lymph glands and her neck. After she was told that her cancer could not be cured through medical help, she came to me for psychotherapy, hoping that perhaps therapy and other modalities of healing could help extend the time she had to live.

Kimi had been given different medications by her doctor, including a variety of hormones. Her doctor admitted that, since there was no known cure for her cancer, she was a kind of guinea pig, and he would try various drugs to see if any might work. Kimi began chemotherapy about the same time that she started psychotherapy. Most people given her diagnosis do not live longer than two years; Kimi, however, survived her fifth year. Here is how she used the seven stages of the Healing Path.

☐ *Awareness* When Kimi first found out that the lump in her breast was malignant, she was shocked; however, with time, she gradually accepted the fact that she had cancer. When her cancer recurred and she was told that it was incurable, she was able to accept the diagnosis, but she had learned through her reading and psychotherapy that she did not have to accept the medical prediction of the time of her death. Being faced with possible death helped Kimi realize how much living she still wanted to do—that she was not yet ready to die. She had made many plans for retirement and was now ready to enjoy some leisure.

Together, Kimi and I questioned whether the stress of her job and the difficulty in finding time to meet her own needs, as well as the needs of others, had had some influence on her becoming sick.

☐ *Meaning* The meaning of her life became a focus of our discussions. She decided that, while well enough, she would be a useful member of society, one with a purpose. Kimi also had her own interests, such as gardening, which she determined to pursue. She told me that "a terminal diagnosis made me consider seriously how I should spend my time and the preciousness of my life."

☐ *Choice* Kimi realized that she had choices, that she did not have to get ready to die, and as soon as she received the diagnosis of recurrence, she realized that she could be doing more to help herself. She reread the Simontons' book, *Getting Well Again*, and started to do the relaxation-imagery exercises it prescribes. Living alone, Kimi knew she that would need her sister's support and gave her a copy of the book. She felt the need for help from a therapist but did nothing about it until her sister pushed her. Kimi became more aware of the difficulty she had in giving to herself and joined my cancer-support group, called by its members the "healing group." She was pleased with herself for taking this step toward health, even though it meant driving to Toronto from out of town each week.

☐ *Will* Kimi realized how much joy there is in life and how much she wanted to go on experiencing it. She had always enjoyed the world of nature, her friends, her work, her church, and now she wanted the joys of retirement. She found that she was definitely not ready to die: in fact, she was determined to live.

☐ *Responsibility* She realized that in some ways she was responsible for her illness. She had never liked confrontation and often backed away from unpleasant situations, hiding her negative feelings. She had great difficulty expressing her emotions to friends and to family, in particular to her sister. In therapy she learned how to express her feelings more readily, and she actually grew much closer to her sister. With the help of others in her therapy group, she became more aware of her right to speak her mind. Kimi actually practiced doing this in the group and consequently found herself much better able to speak her mind to the medical profession: she was finally able to cancel some scheduled X rays and to insist on less chemotherapy. This was a real achievement for Kimi and improved her self-confidence.

☐ *Strategies* The strategies that Kimi used to improve her health included relaxation and imagery techniques, individual and group therapy, a macrobiotic diet, therapeutic touch, prayer, acceptance of support from friends and relatives, involvement in projects and volunteer work, and acceptance of medical help.

☐ *Change* Each and every day Kimi felt extremely grateful to be alive. She did not want to waste any precious time and gave herself goals to reach at certain intervals. She chose activities that really interested her rather than going to meetings and activities out of a sense of duty. She felt she was in closer touch with her friends and family and wanted very much to maintain this contact.

The message of her illness was twofold. The first was to be more aware of her own needs: by caring more for herself, she was better able to give to others, and by giving to others she added to her own well-being. The second was her increased awareness of the importance of purpose to health. Kimi felt positive about her service work with, for example, Amnesty International, and about her contribution to an outreach committee at her church. Her group had been successful in bringing out a refugee family from El Salvador.

It was exciting to share in Kimi's journey to health.

As her chemotherapy treatments progressed, it was sad to see her hair fall out and her color become so sallow. It was, however, great fun to be part of her experience in choosing a wig. And then, it was even more fun to discover with her, as she became bald, that she had an exquisitely shaped head. Thereafter, in all the therapy sessions, she was asked not to wear her wig so that we could enjoy the beauty of her head. Kimi, feeling so warmly received and cared for, was delighted to co-operate.

Then we had the most exciting experience. As Kimi's psychotherapy progressed, her lumps began to diminish. Even her doctors were startled. She was faithfully doing her healing imagery, and in therapy we were looking for any unconscious factors that might be at work and in some way inhibiting her health. Gradually every lump disappeared. Kimi was ecstatic, and so were the rest of us in the group—this was encouragement for everybody regarding his or her own ability to heal. One lump had been pressing on Kimi's voice box, making her voice barely audible. Her doctor had said this would probably be a permanent disability. Imagine our delight as her voice grew stronger each week and was finally normal.

Kimi was relatively content with her experiences with the medical profession, with the exception of her first oncologist, who would not explain to her what was really happening concerning her cancer. This lack of understanding and concern for how she was feeling about her illness left Kimi confused, uncertain, and afraid. Her second oncologist was much more compassionate. Neither doctor could predict the effectiveness of the chemotherapy treatments, but nevertheless recommended them. Both knew that she was in psychotherapy and seemed surprised at her improving health. Her second doctor eventually had the insight to credit her remarkable recovery to "your spirit, your determination, your will to live, and your faith."

I wrote to this doctor, asking for a copy of Kimi's medical record and telling him about my plans to write this book. I never heard from him, nor would he release Kimi's medical records to Kimi herself. Whose life is it, anyway?

☐ MARY JEAN CHAMP

Mary Jean Champ is an attractive, energetic, healthy-looking divorcée in her mid-fifties who for many years had a demanding job in publishing. She is also the mother of two adult children.

She had a relatively early awakening to the fallibility of the medical profession when she was twenty-six years old. She was told that, because of an abnormally high sedimentation rate, she had developed a form of fast-moving arthritis and would be a cripple by the time she was thirty. Despair and hopelessness overwhelmed Mary Jean as she accepted her doctor's description of her destiny. For a short while she gave up on her health, but introspective thinking led her to a growing awareness of her life force, and she eventually decided that becoming a cripple would not be part of her future and has not been troubled seriously with arthritis since that time.

Some years later, Mary Jean ran into difficulty with alcohol. Feeling desperate, she sought medical advise, but her doctor treated her as if she were an infant—with a pat on the head, tranquilizers, and platitudes such as "There, there, now why is a nice girl like you thinking she's an alcoholic? All you have to do is simply not drink so much." Feeling unheard, misunderstood, and very confused, Mary Jean "hit bottom" and gave up.

Mary Jean's giving up was the result of her misconception that, if there was no one "out there" who could solve her problems, including God, then there was no hope. She remained in a deep depression for some time, but even the darkest void can become a source of light if we open our eyes to alternatives. After a four-day "blackout," she joined Alcoholics Anonymous and experienced a profound spiritual awakening, becoming aware of a healing force or power that had nothing to do with medicine. Her consciousness of this energy continued to grow during the twelve years she was a member of Alcoholics Anonymous.

Mary Jean was referred to me for psychotherapy by another member of A.A. who knew she was hoping to learn how to express her frustration and anger in more productive and satisfying ways. During this time she discovered that Hedda, a close friend, had cancer. I recommended that she give Hedda *Getting Well Again* and urge her friend to do what she could to help herself. Mary Jean's next move up the consciousness scale came when she witnessed how effective these self-help exercises were for Hedda.

Mary Jean's major problem was that she would not take enough time, energy, and responsibility for her own health, for herself. She even asked me point-blank one day, "Sheila, is it going to take a diagnosis of cancer to make me take care of myself?" I had the nerve to say, "Maybe it is, Mary Jean." Several weeks later she came crying into my office with the news that she had been diagnosed with breast cancer. She was finally ready to work on herself.

☐ *Awareness* Mary Jean became aware that there is a spiritual power that comes through other people, from a higher place, and from within oneself. She believes in the potency of this power. She also realized, with amazement, that she herself could make her own choices, that there were various healing alternatives to medicine in which she could invest her time, energy, and money.

☐ *Meaning* She learned that the meaning in her life would not just appear, or be given to her by somebody else, but rather would come from what she put into her life and the lives of others. Mary Jean stated, "The joy of finding meaning in my life—the unbelievable fact that I am again an artist—the most profound meaning in my life now—came gradually, during and after the cancer."

☐ *Choice* For Mary Jean, choice meant that she could take control of her own disease and decide to live—or she could let herself slip into despair and die. It was a difficult decision for her to make, but she knew that her fate was in her hands. I reminded her to take herself more seriously, to value who she really was and could become. She heard me. She spent a week at her cottage with Hedda, struggling with her life-and-death urges, and finally, for the first time, made a conscious decision to live.

☐ *Will* Mary Jean's will was galvanized into action following her decision to live. Action is encouraged by defining some future goals for oneself, and Mary Jean discovered that she did not have any. No wonder she was feeling like a non-person! In a positive rage for not caring more about her life, she exclaimed, "I *am* going to live!" That was the point at which she decided to get on with her life and, as she reached out for help, her will to live became translated into her will to act.

☐ *Responsibility* For Mary Jean, the hardest part of her journey was learning to be responsible for herself and her health. She has found it difficult to keep from backsliding, from repeating old patterns and self-defeating behavior. For example, she would find herself indulging in self-pity, repressing her true feelings, or lashing out in anger rather than taking time to identify what she really needed from someone and expressing her need to that person. She realizes that she has to constantly work at being healthy, transferring the positive attitude and belief in self and action that were helpful when she had cancer to any other illness or difficult situation that might arise. She has sought out people, books, articles, and healing methods that can show her alternatives to medicine.

☐ *Strategies* Mary Jean's first strategy was to do her own research on what was known medically about breast surgery. She then went about interviewing oncologists. She came across one arrogant and ignorant surgeon who strongly suggested that she have her breast removed completely because, he stated, she would not like the appearance of her breast after a lumpectomy. She finally found a surgeon who did not impose his thinking on her but instead listened to her wishes; through a mutual decision they achieved a successful lumpectomy.

Mary Jean concentrated on individual and group therapy. She gave a great deal to others and, in so doing, grew within herself immeasurably. She practiced relaxation and imagery, investigated the pros and cons of hypnotism and the macrobiotic diet, and exercised more than usual. She studied Jungian psychology and included time for spiritual growth as part of her regular life. She left her successful middle-management job in publishing and is happily earning her living as a watercolorist and art consultant, something she always wanted to do.

☐ *Change* Mary Jean accepted people into her life in a way that she had not experienced before. She learned about interdependence. She discovered that she had healing energy that she could share with others. She learned to take charge and to become more accepting of difficult circumstances and of other people.

The most important change that Mary Jean made was to free her creative talent. She had successfully repressed her artistic gift for almost twenty-two years, unnecessarily turning her creative energy into destructive behavior. At last she returned to her love of art and enrolled in painting classes.

It seems paradoxical that her illness helped her to discover her spiritual power. This power, when translated into action, became a direct expression of Mary Jean in the form of painting. She acknowledged to me, "Every time I pick up the paintbrush, I choose life."

Mary Jean was given her diagnosis of breast cancer in June of 1982. The lumpectomy followed. Six years later, she remains clear of cancer.

☐ *VICTORIA STRAUSS*

Victoria Strauss is a remarkable and lovable woman in her mid-forties. She is philosophic in her thinking and has a wonderful sense of humor. After earning a Ph.D. from the University of Toronto in music she was employed by the faculty of music for many years. At present she is the education co-ordinator and chief writer for the Education Manual for the

Canadian Artist Series, a project of the Canadian Music Education Association (CMEA). She also does freelance work, such as conducting, adjudicating, and teaching. Victoria heard that I was the psychotherapist for a number of cancer patients, helping them to discover and use their own resources for healing, and decided that she needed to reassess her own emotional health. She began psychotherapy in 1984, although her history of cancer extends back to 1960.

In 1960 Victoria was diagnosed with cancer of the rectum. She went through the surgical procedure of a colostomy, and the operation was considered medically successful. Twenty-four years later during a routine examination, it was discovered that she had a very low hemoglobin level and signs of occult blood (a symptom of cancer). On March 1, 1984, her surgeon removed a growth in her lower intestine. On March 8 she was diagnosed with cancer of the uterus, and in April a dilation and curettage revealed cancerous cells in her cervix. She was referred to Princess Margaret Hospital in Toronto for radiation therapy: twenty-four treatments aimed at the tailbone area. At the same time Victoria was working hard in therapy, visualizing the cancerous cells being sloughed off and carried away. It was great news to hear, in July, that her tests and examination showed her cervix to be clear of cancerous cells. However, this was soon followed with the discouraging news that her oncologist recommended a hysterectomy. In January 1985 the surgery was performed successfully, and since then all pathology reports have been clear, indicating no sign of cancer. The internal work that Victoria has done on herself is truly amazing, with the result, I believe, that she has retrieved her life.

The following description shows the use that she made of the theory and stages of the Healing Path.

☐ *Awareness* Victoria became aware that cancer was not just a physical illness but a symbol of her life and the sickness that was within—a mental, spiritual, and emotional malady. She wanted to learn more about the connection between her illness and her emotional makeup.

Research has indicated that serious loss in the life of the cancer personality can bring about despair. The typical pattern indicates that within one or two years after loss the first signs of cancer may appear. Victoria's story verified this concept. When she was told that she was to be denied tenure at the university, she entered a period of "black despair." She would close her eyes and see no shapes, figures, or colors—only blackness. She actually felt that she had come to the end of her life. She also had to have her dog, her companion of eighteen years, put to sleep. The following year Victoria began to find that she had very little energy and she had trouble getting her breath. She knew that something was dreadfully wrong, but fear kept her from making an appointment with her doctor for quite some time.

When Victoria received her second diagnosis, her immediate reaction was a combination of shock and gratitude. The shock was not from the discovery that she had cancer but that it was recurring after twenty-four years. She experienced overwhelming gratitude for those intervening years of health. Her thankfulness was so much in evidence that she was not aware of feelings of anger. She has been in touch with her anger only since she has become well again.

☐ *Meaning* To Victoria, her cancer assumed proportions far beyond the actual physical symptoms and medical diagnosis. Her question was not "why me, Lord?" but "why NOW, Lord?" Her need to search for and find personal meaning in her illness was imperative. She remembered that following her first bout with cancer she had made a covenant with God: if she were allowed to live, she would live a life of purpose and value. The diagnosis felt to Victoria like a signal that in some ways she was not keeping her part in this bargain as well as she could. This message was very meaningful to her and caused her to re-evaluate her life.

☐ *Choice* Victoria chose to co-operate with the medical profession and to derive as much benefit from it as she could. At the same time she decided to continue her psychotherapy, to continue discovering and understanding the destructive forces within her that were obviously manifesting themselves physically. She discovered that she was full of emotion but ill-equipped to use these emotions in her own defense. Her terror of the negative within herself was greater than her fear of cancer.

She was grateful for the opportunity to use Gestalt therapy and psychodrama to act out her choice for life in concert with a fellow member of our cancer support group, Mary Jean Champ. By bringing her negative death wish out into the open, Victoria was able to confront it and accept it as part of herself. She found out that, although her black despair was strong and would probably always be a part of her, it did not match the strength of her desire and will for life, her positive forces.

☐ *Will* Victoria's will to live was and is very strong. She realized that if she were to live a happy, contented, and productive life, she would have to change both inwardly and outwardly. She translated her will into an active search for a spiritual identification with God. She combined her will with the will of God, and hand in hand they recovered her strength and courage. Her prayers were simple, honest, and, she believes, effective.

☐ *Responsibility* Victoria took the concept of being responsible for her health and illness in both mind and body very seriously. She read a great deal and asked her doctors many questions about her treatment and options. She participated in individual and group therapy, learning how to reach out to friends for help. Victoria recognized her cancer personality (see Chapter 12) and the crucial need to change some aspects of it and to maintain constant alertness to the destructive aspects of that personality. She appreciated the importance of her spiritual connection and took the necessary steps to renew this.

When Victoria heard the news that her cervix was cancer-free, she was filled with joy but not surprised. She had taken the responsibility of visualizing away the weak, sick cells and felt that she had been effective.

☐ *Strategies* Victoria established her values and priorities through her strategies. Her first priority was to achieve a rich spiritual life with God, her soul, and a sense of peace at her center. She recovered a veneration of God, whom she experienced as a powerful force or presence. While in hospital, she never felt alone and credits her spiritual connection with keeping her together throughout her hospital ordeals. Her seeking out and opening herself to a power larger than herself gave her a sense of calm and balance.

Music is a tremendous emotional support for her. Music is her career, her soul, her hobby, her joy; it even affects her self-worth and image. She took her tapes to the hospital and listened to them often:

Mozart, Bach, and Strauss were her constant companions. She was delighted to discover the importance of music to Pablo Casals and Albert Schweitzer in their times of need. Music made her feel happy deep inside, and she recommends it highly for anyone with any illness.

Victoria realized the importance of continuing therapy in order to keep clearing away psychological problems. She has accepted her cancer and has no desire to hide the fact of it. It is extremely important for her and others to realize that cancer is not synonymous with death. She verbalized her fears, met them head on, and dealt with them. She recognized her tendency to stoicism and self-retreat and is gradually changing this. She came to the understanding that I, her therapist, really cared about her, and she gradually learned to trust me. Initially held back in wonderment at the honesty of interaction and the power of the group process, she became warmed by the other women, felt their caring, and was drawn into the group. When we held hands and breathed together, she found the transmission of strength palpable. The group was able to help Victoria during her radiation treatments. When she climbed up on the table for her first treatment, she was so frightened that her teeth chattered. I suggested in group that she lie down in the middle of our circle and that the other women give to her by touching her physically and feeling for her. Victoria found this strange at first but was trusting enough to be able to receive their gifts. The next time she submitted to a radiation treatment she had the sense of the presence of the group, her teeth did not chatter, and she felt more peaceful. Her relationships with her mother, her friends, and her acquaintances have shifted: she can now let them give to her.

Victoria has discovered that her contacts with people are crucial for her health. This applies not only to close friends and acquaintances but also to strangers. When a friend told Mary Jean Champ that Victoria was sick, Mary Jean bought a copy of *Getting Well Again* and visited her, asking her to read the book. Victoria was astonished that a seeming stranger could care about her so much, and after Mary Jean's visit, Victoria felt hopeful and was able to start to put her life back together. She is amazed at the powerful influence people can have on one another and has derived great benefits from letting down her defenses, opening up to people, and letting them touch her emotionally.

One of her strategies is to devote more time to the things that give her pleasure. Reading and stimulating her sense of humor are two of the most important activities, and she has reread ten of Stephen Leacock's books. Immediate pleasure far outweighs the long-term goals that used to rule her life, and she is much easier on herself.

Victoria's pets are a continuing source of satisfaction, providing a healthy emotional outlet for her. She hopes someday to write about them, to describe what loving animals has taught her about herself and about being human.

Victoria found imagery to be an effective tool. She was able to get rid of her headaches by visualization and decided to apply the technique to her uterus. She visualized her white blood cells as an army of Russian crusaders, all dressed in white, fully armed, and mounted on huge chargers, with banners and pinions floating high. Situated on a hill, looking over enemy terrain, they had the obvious advantage in size, number, and strategies, as well as military tactics. She amused herself by imagining that this was a Cecil B. deMille production, with a cast of thousands shouting their enthusiasm. Her army was ready to attack. She would march the crusaders through the back wall of her uterus, through the outside lining of the wall, and into the internal walls of her uterus. She was shocked at an image of a densely wooded forest that arose unbidden from her unconscious: her army hacked and chopped but the enormity and the hopelessness of the job were overwhelming. It was at this point that Victoria realized how much negativity was in her unconscious.

She brought this experience into group and was able to create a dialogue between her positive and negative forces, between life and death. This process gave her valuable insight and strength and provided the clue that had been blocking her. She returned home, feeling some relief, and started to visualize again. This time she saw her uterus as a large geodesic dome. Victoria, as Dr. Strauss, was to run a project with the help of technicians and scientists working in their white lab coats. Inside was the command post and outside was a system for runoff liquid, an association with her discharge. The walls of the dome were healthy red tissue. Teams of technicians were using laser beams to irradiate gray cancerous cells that had collected, and as the gray dissolved, the technicians would use hoses to clean off the surface of the dome. From her command post Victoria gave pep talks, emphasizing the importance of the job they were doing, telling them to change shifts every four hours, and urging them to work to their utmost capacity even though she might not be present. Their goal was to achieve a bright, clean, interior for the dome, followed by a very special concert at which Victoria was to be the star. This image had great power and significance for her, and she used it consistently.

☐ *Change* One of the most significant changes in Victoria is her awareness of her growing strength, and part of this is the result of change in her relationships with people. It still amazes her that her friends, relatives, students, and colleagues want to "rock her in the cradle of their good wishes." She has developed a strong sense of the helping nature of people. She describes her change as profound and she enjoys her new state of mind and feelings.

She has faced her own possible death twice and has come through these experiences transformed. Her priorities have shifted from valuing herself as an academic with degrees and professional accomplishments to seeing herself as a human being with a surprising number of admirable personal traits. Having successfully faced death, she is now able to look at life with the same degree of courage, determination, and staying power that she had when she marshaled the troops against her cancer. Depression, anger, and low self-worth are still malingerers, but Victoria now has a set of strategies with which to combat these diseases of the mind.

She does not know what her future holds or how long her life will be. She finds it curious that not knowing and not making long-term plans help to make her feel free. Her economic security is uncertain, but this seems a minor concern to her when compared to the fact that she knows that her strengths and faith will be with her to the end.

There is an encouraging epilogue for Victoria. A while ago, she began to bleed vaginally and once again was sent to the hospital. The oncologists who examined her decided to treat the incident as a recurrence of cancer. Victoria bravely told them that she was 99 percent certain that she did not have cancer and requested that they run all the preliminary tests on her before beginning treatment. The tests indicated that she is completely cancer-free—her bleeding had been caused by a lesion.

The three cancer clients I have described above opted for medical treatment combined with psychotherapy. The following cancer clients rejected medical treatment and chose psychotherapy along with other alternative healing methods.

☐ SUZANNE HAMEL

Suzanne Hamel is a beautiful, vivacious, thirty-year-old French Canadian who is presently employed as a buyer for one of the top fashion lines of women's clothing. At the time of her diagnosis she had no job, had just broken up with her boyfriend, and was feeling emotionally drained. Her yearly Pap smear indicated cancerous cells in her cervix, and Suzanne agreed to have a cone biopsy done for the purpose of removing the diseased cells. Further analysis of her tissues indicated that the cancer cells extended too far into her uterus to be removed with a further biopsy. Her doctor gave her two options: a radical hysterectomy or radiation treatment. He strongly recommended the former, but Suzanne is looking forward to marriage and having babies and the idea of having her ovaries removed was unacceptable. She told the doctor that she needed some time to think the matter over and would let him know her decision. She told me that her doctor seemed shocked and annoyed that she would not book a date for the operation immediately. A few weeks later Suzanne received her registration, or booking, for her operation in the mail. The doctor had gone ahead and scheduled a hysterectomy without her authorization. Needless to say, this made her very angry. She made appointments with a few other doctors to confirm the diagnosis. They were all in agreement that she should have a hysterectomy.

Suzanne found a source of strength within herself that enabled her to discover her own path to health.

She listened to medical advice, considered it carefully, ultimately rejected it, and opened herself up to alternative methods of healing. At a seminar on self-healing, she was introduced to books and ideas that provided new ways of looking at her health. One of these books was *Joy's Way*, a book by W. Brugh Joy that describes our potential for healing with body energy. Following this seminar, Suzanne felt that something dormant in her had awakened and that her rebirth had begun.

A stranger at the seminar suggested that she call me, and it was at this juncture that Suzanne began psychotherapy. Finding my office an emotionally safe place, she openly shared her fears, anxieties, and deepest thoughts. She felt that she unloaded "a lot of garbage." She cried and cried throughout each session as we uncovered long-hidden guilt feelings; she began to re-establish her connection with God and the universe. She realized the necessity of balancing her spirituality, her psychological makeup, and her physiology. She found these sessions fulfilling and described her body as feeling "light" after each session.

The seven steps of the Healing Path helped her in her journey to health.

☐ *Awareness* Suzanne realized that she was out of touch with her body. Some of her negative experiences with doctors helped her to realize the importance of reconnecting with and valuing her body. She became aware that she had not been answering her physical, emotional, and spiritual needs and discovered that she could choose what seemed right for her. She learned that there were other, nonmedical ways to heal herself.

☐ *Meaning* Suzanne realized that illness does not just happen, that there must be some meaning in disease. She found that a big part of her disease was related to certain things that she had been repressing or blocking out for years, incidents around which she had built feelings of guilt or anger. Rather than express these feelings, she had denied them. What she needed to do now was to accept them and forgive herself. The strongest message from her disease was "It's time to wake up."

☐ *Choice* The most influential and powerful choice that Suzanne made was to choose her own method of healing. She chose to use her mind as a tool for healing and to work on developing harmony between her mind-body-spirit. She also chose to ask God for spiritual help. She chose to find out what foods would be best for her and to change her eating habits and decided to make time every day for meditation.

☐ *Will* Suzanne questioned her motivation to live: was her life worth all this anxiety, time, and energy? She became aware that, yes, she wanted to live very much; but she also knew that she would have to make some dramatic changes in her lifestyle if she hoped to recover and maintain her health. She realized that she had not been living a healthy life, that it was time for her to confront some emotional issues that she had been avoiding. She would have to slow down the pace of her life, make her days less stressful, and learn how to ask for help. Suzanne resolved to take action in dealing with these problems and make the necessary changes.

☐ *Responsibility* Suzanne was struck with the profundity of the realization that no other person could be responsible for the recovery of her health, that it was up to *her* to accomplish her healing. She feels grateful to her cancer for acting as a catalyst and helping her gain this lifesaving insight. Because she is unique, she alone had to choose the direction that was right for her. She searched, listened, and read all the information she could obtain.

She was determined to listen to the messages from her body. She realized she had been abusing her health and that her body had sent her signals in the past to which she had never listened. "Now," she said, "the buzzer is sounding loud and clear."

Suzanne visited a doctor who is also a naturopath. He confirmed the existence of her cancer and, through his enlightened discourse, helped her open doors she did not know existed. She realized how out of touch with the universe she had become. He helped her to feel that she had a significant role to play in her illness and health. Suzanne left his office feeling as though a heavy weight had been lifted from her chest; she also had a strong sense that she was on the road to recovery.

☐ *Strategies* In addition to individual psychotherapy, naturopathy, healing seminars, and reading as strategies on her journey to health, Suzanne also joined our healing group. She found that the other members of the group shared her feelings on what it is like to have cancer, and she received the necessary support to help heal herself. The group members helped one another discover how to bring harmony into and re-establish control over their lives. Suzanne says she is grateful that she had a place to go where she felt safe, a place where she knew that she would not be judged, but rather cared for and encouraged. She believes that her therapy helped a great deal with her recovery.

Visualization proved to be another successful strategy. Suzanne would make time twice every day to be in a quiet environment and would then practice deep breathing, relaxing each part of her body. She would visualize her body getting rid of the cancerous cells in various ways. She would almost always find that she needed to urinate after this meditation, and again, at that time, she visualized all the diseased cells being flushed away from her body.

Suzanne changed her eating habits drastically. She decided to eat according to the dictates of a macrobiotic diet. This is an extremely restricted diet, consisting chiefly of whole grains and vegetables. Its purpose is to promote health and well-being. Suzanne loves it, believes it to be extremely effective for her, and uses it constantly.

☐ *Change* Suzanne made some extreme changes in her lifestyle. She lost a few friends who could not understand where she was coming from or where she was going. She, however, feels that she is living in the best way for her well-being and will not be discouraged from her journey to health. She reminds herself constantly to slow down and not push herself so hard. She takes time to enjoy herself and be grateful for her life.

Suzanne returned to her doctor two years later for her annual checkup. Even though he could find absolutely no sign of cancer, he continued to strongly recommend that she have a hysterectomy. She asked for the release of her medical files, and he refused to give them to her. She was amazed that he would continue to insist on the operation when there was no evidence of cancer and has consequently changed to another doctor.

Five years have passed since her diagnosis. Other doctors have confirmed that Suzanne no longer has cancer, and she never did have the operation. 'She believes that surgery might have appeared to solve the problem temporarily but that the cancer would have reappeared. It was her mind-body-spirit that needed healing. Her cancer was only a symptom of a much larger problem.

Suzanne realizes how powerful her inner resources for healing were and still are. She hopes that others will have the strength to follow their own wisdom. She also hopes for increased public awareness of alternative ways to deal with disease. She believes that we have within ourselves all we need to cure ourselves. The secret is to listen to our inner voice and then take action.

☐ LAURIE BERTON

Laurie Berton is an intelligent, energetic, gorgeous woman of twenty-nine. When I met her, she was a dental technician and called herself the tooth fairy. She was diagnosed with Hodgkin's disease, a malignant cancer of the lymphatic tissues usually characterized by the enlargement of a group of lymph nodes. The liver, spleen, bone marrow, and bones may also be involved. She had heard about the kind of psychotherapy I was conducting with cancer clients and wished to participate. She came for psychotherapy, wanting to learn more about herself and how she could heal herself.

When her G.P. explained to her the results of her medical tests, Laurie was devastated. It seemed as though the doctor was not really talking to her at all. She felt nauseated, then started to shake and cry profusely. The medical treatments suggested to her were surgery, radiation, and chemotherapy, but Laurie saw these treatments as invasive and did not want any of her healthy tissues destroyed. After careful consideration, she rejected them all, preferring to try a more natural method of healing. The following is an account of how Laurie used the stages of the Healing Path to achieve health.

☐ *Awareness* One of the first effects of this crisis was that Laurie became aware of how little she knew about her own physiology. She began to read everything she could find on the subject of cancer and, at the same time, began to discover how her body worked and why disease occurs. She wanted to understand how she could affect the process of disease or health.

Laurie also became aware of how closely she associated cancer with death. The two words seemed practically synonymous. She was terrified, feeling that she might die within a few weeks.

☐ *Meaning* Bewildered as to why this was happening to her, Laurie searched diligently for some sort of meaning to her illness. During her therapy, as she looked back over her life, she realized that at some point she had put a wall around herself. It was a "cement" defense that she had needed at the time. When she was younger she had moved to Canada from England and had said good-bye to the people she loved most—her grandparents—but she also had felt that she was saying good-bye to her childhood. She had felt she had to be "big" now, that there was no more time for fun, play, and childish emotions. Her outlets for self-expression had closed down. She remembers concentrating on all the "right" things to do. She had continued to feel small and rigid, holding on tightly, keeping herself in control. Laurie found the message in her illness to be that she needed to let down and let go, to give herself enough space and freedom to let life in. She had been suffocating.

☐ *Choice* It was very clear to Laurie that she could let her disease take over her life (an unhealthy physical manifestation of her control) or she could heal herself. After careful consideration she chose not to avail herself of medical help but rather to learn about and use alternative healing methods. Laurie chose to live.

☐ *Will* Other than being a little tired, Laurie did not even feel sick. She was determined to continue living as if she were not sick. She was so thankful just to be alive that she could not keep still. While in hospital for diagnostic tests, she walked and walked the hallways.

The diagnosis tuned Laurie into the importance of her life and her strong desire to overcome any obstacle. She decided, in no uncertain terms, that she *would do anything* so that she might have her life. Laurie decided not to die.

☐ *Responsibility* Laurie realized that, in order to take responsibility for herself, she must find her inner strength. To be honest with herself became her first priority. Then she began asking questions, searching for the right path to take on her journey to health, and discovered there were many ways in which she could help to heal herself.

☐ *Strategies* After investigating the macrobiotic diet, Laurie chose to use a modified version of it that suited her tastes. She also cleansed her body with herbal remedies and lots of exercise.

She worked hard in therapy, gaining insight and understanding as to why and how she had armored herself against the world. She was able to translate what she learned into action and to build closer and more effective relationships with her family and friends.

She meditated often and learned the techniques of visualization. She concentrated on creating "a joyful existence" for herself. She realized the importance of the mind-body-spirit relationship and successfully pursued a connection with an energy force that was greater and more powerful than herself. And she opened herself, with gratitude, to guidance and support.

☐ *Change* The most significant change for Laurie has been awakening to her feelings and realizing how they affect her body. She was unaware that she had a "tough outside" and a "soft center," and she has been successful at integrating these two parts of herself. Laurie feels that her outside and inside now mesh rather than clash.

She has discovered a joy in life that she never knew could exist. She has experienced this joy on a mountaintop on a clear, cold morning and on a sailboat on the ocean under a full moon. Sometimes she feels as if she is pure essence, without a physical body, just absorbing the life around her.

Five years have passed since Laurie was given her diagnosis. She now has no sign of Hodgkin's disease. She lives very much in the present and is currently a ski instructor in the Laurentian Mountains.

Laurie has some constructive criticism for the medical profession. She said her doctors would not answer all her concerns and made her feel stupid because she refused radiation. Laurie feels very angry that her intelligence was questioned, that she was supposed to simply let her doctors take control of her body and mind. She was told that "young and intelligent patients are the most difficult to treat."

She found the treatment she received from the medical profession to be completely impersonal. For example, her blood-test results were read out loud over a P.A. system to a crowded waiting room at the hospital.

Laurie believes that her doctors were treating only her symptoms, with no regard for her as a whole person. At no time did they suggest that there was any alternative to traditional treatment, on any level, be it physiological, psychological, or spiritual. If Laurie had not searched for herself, she would have been unaware that she had any choices.

Laurie says now, "Would I be here, in the Laurentians, skiing on the mountains every day, if I had not been diagnosed as having cancer? Definitely not!" Based on her own experience, Laurie believes that everybody should have at least one major life crisis to help them find out who they really are and where they are going. She says with a chuckle that "cancer was the best thing that ever happened to me!"

☐ OTHER CLIENTS

Although the concept of the Healing Path was developed from the experiences of terminally ill cancer patients who healed themselves, many of my other clients with various symptoms and illnesses have also used the seven stages of the Healing Path successfully. They include people with alcoholic problems, those who have suffered heart attacks, people with recurring boils, rashes, allergies, asthma, back pain, migraine headaches, and even arthritis.

I believe that most noninfectious illness is psychogenic in origin; that is, that the seeds of illness originate in the mind, usually on an unconscious level.

I had a client in his middle teens, Robbie Forman, a handsome, gangly young man. He came to see me because of anxiety attacks and terrible migraine headaches. His autocratic father was uncomfortable with talk of emotions and feelings and suspicious of therapy. One time, when Robbie suffered a particularly acute episode of migraine, Mr. Forman insisted that his son be admitted to hospital. I visited Robbie there and found him extremely unhappy about being hospitalized; together we conspired for his release. I felt a little like an intruder but was trying to provide Robbie with the support he needed. His doctors had already tried various kinds of medication, with no apparent success. They had even suggested ECT, electroconvulsive therapy, whereby a convulsion is produced by passing an electric current through the brain. I pleaded with Robbie's parents not to consent to this barbaric form of treatment. All this time Robbie and I were trying to uncover the major sources of stress in his life, and we were slowly succeeding.

The lack of communication between his mother and father and between his parents and himself was bothering him tremendously. Robbie was questioning the unwritten rules of his family. One of these confusing rules was that you do not express what you are really feeling; you say what you think others want to hear. There was no place where Robbie could feel safe enough to express his anguish and feel heard. No wonder his head was aching! Robbie and I convinced his parents that he should check out of the hospital because treatment there was having no effect.

The first step for Robbie was to make his own decision and tell his parents what was right for him. He became *aware* that I cared about him, that he could open up to me, and that there were other *choices* besides hospitals, medication, and being sick. He began to see the *meaning* in his migraine. He understood now that it was time for him to take control of his life and make his own decisions. He was *willing* to do some intensive therapeutic work and take *responsibility* for developing *strategies* to help him make the necessary changes in his life. I remember the day he was ready to give up his headache. He did some deep breathing, relaxed his body, and then literally put his head in my hands and let me take his migraine headache from him. We both looked at each other in amazement. Robbie had healed himself with a little help from his therapist. Robbie's mother and brother also came into therapy, which helped Robbie, helped them, and facilitated the total family interaction.

My experience with Robbie took place more than five years ago—he has not had a migraine headache since.

Another client of mine, David Snowdon, a pastor in a fairly large church, was diagnosed as having extensive diverticulitis in the lower bowel. It was also discovered that he had large cysts in his kidneys and multiple cysts on his liver. This diagnosis made David examine the *meaning* and direction his health and therefore his life were taking. He gradually became *aware* that he had been very unhappy for years, but had been bluffing his way through. He made the *choice* to be honest about his life. He felt that if he became increasingly ill he would die without ever having really lived.

David found within himself a great urgency, or *will*, to live. He felt, however, that in some ways illness and death would be the easier route. Life would mean taking *responsibility* for who he really was and what he really wanted to do. He wanted to leave the parish ministry and to develop a private counseling practice. He had wanted to leave his marriage of thirty years. He knew that he would have to deal with community dissatisfaction but felt this action to be necessary for the honest fulfillment of his life.

His *strategies* were to trust in his relationship with his Creator, to receive support from Jesus, and to obtain some psychotherapy. He purchased a bicycle to help him get back in touch with his physical energy.

His feelings of hopelessness are gone, and his thought processes are clearer than they have ever been. He has lost weight, can feel his body changing as he comes to terms with his conflicting emotions, and is optimistic and happy. He describes himself as "growing into wellness."

David was recently accused of having had a facelift. "No," he said, "I have simply taken off my mask."

☐ 12
THE CONNECTION BETWEEN MIND AND BODY

There is now incontrovertible evidence that mankind has just entered upon the greatest period of change the world has ever known. The ills from which we are suffering have had their seat in the very foundation of human thought.—Pierre Teilhard de Chardin

The connection between illness and psychological makeup has been known for almost two thousand years. Why then, in the practice of modern medicine, is the treatment of physical manifestation of disease so rarely conducted alongside a consideration of the psychological condition?

In the late nineteenth and the early twentieth centuries, when the emerging sciences of psychology and psychiatry were developing tools to examine the link between illness and the mind, medical science was drawing inspiration from the mechanical triumphs of the Industrial Revolution. As a result of this fundamental difference in approach, a deep gulf arose between medical and psychological thinking.

Today, while medical literature indicates exceptional progress in inventing and refining physical therapies and surgical procedures, it generally exhibits a noticeable lack of interest in the emotional, mental, and spiritual experiences of patients. Spontaneous remission remains unexplained and often ignored, as do major individual differences in response to treatment.

The psychological literature describes emotional states related to illness but in general fails to suggest any physiological mechanisms to explain the relationship. The ways in which individuals themselves affect the course of their health and illness have remained relatively unexplored. Notwithstanding, a few branches of psychological and medical research do shed light on the *profound connection between psychological states and disease.* Current research of this type includes that concerned with (1) the effects of the emotions on physiological functions, (2) the significance of attitudes and beliefs on health, (3) the effects of stress on the immune system, (4) the role of the body as metaphor for psychological health, and (5) the applications of biofeedback research in self-healing.

Psychoneuroimmunology is the name applied to the study of the relationship between emotions and health. It is today common knowledge that negative emotions and experiences can affect health and complicate medical treatment, making one susceptible to various diseases ranging from the common cold to cancer; the psychosomatic (relating to mental and physical factors) basis for ulcers, asthma, and migraine headaches received acknowledgment from most in the medical profession some time ago. Also, evidence indicating a predisposition to heart attacks among highly stressed individuals has brought added respect to the concept of psychosomatic involvement in life-threatening diseases.

Psychosomatic illness, however, has until recently generally been attributed to mental processes, such as memories, motives, and intentions, that are held not to be accessible to the individual's awareness. It is now being discovered that a change in outlook and attitude can enhance the body's natural healing system. The degree to which one might consciously influence the mind to heal the body is becoming the subject of intense research among a few enlightened scientists. A leader in this new field, Professor A. Cunningham, defines disease as "any persistent harmful disturbance of equilibrium." The three interrelating subsystems that maintain this equilibrium are known as the *nervous* (i.e., brain and spinal cord), *endocrine* (i.e., hormones), and *immune* systems. Our developing knowledge of the power of the mind to effect physiological change in the body offers promise to anyone afflicted with any disease affected by one's psychological makeup.

The following information illuminates the role that individuals play in determining the course or direction of their health or illness. While much of this material relates to cancer, the physiological dynamics are applicable to any disease with a psychological component.

□ THE EFFECT OF EMOTIONS ON ILLNESS

As early as 1959, Dr. Eugene Pendergrass, in his presidential speech to the American Cancer Society, emphasized the importance of treating not only the physical manifestations of cancer but the patient as a whole:

> There is solid evidence that the course of disease in general is affected by emotional distress ... thus we, as doctors, may begin to emphasize *treatment of the patient as a whole*, as well as of the disease from which he is suffering.... It is my sincere hope ... that within one's mind is a power capable of exerting forces which can either enhance or inhibit the progress of disease. [Emphasis mine]

The great physicians of the past believed that emotions and disease were interrelated. Galen, the Greek physician who lived from A.D. 129 to ca. 199, suggested that melancholy women suffered more from cancer than sanguine women. In 1402, a physician wrote that

> to get angry and shout keeps up the natural heat or bodily energies of man and relieves stress, but what displeases me is your being grieved and taking all manners to heart, for it is this, as the whole of physics teaches, which destroys our body more than any other cause.

In 1846, Dr. Walter Walshe in *The Nature and Treatment of Cancer* stated emphatically that mental disquietude was a basis for cancer and that those who had a family history of this disease should avoid the stressful professions of the bar, medicine, and diplomacy, but that the army, navy, and the church were safe. The implicit suggestion that health follows from obedience to hierarchical authority is highly questionable, but the claim for a relationship between stress and cancer has been shown to be correct.

Conducted just before the turn of the century, one of the first statistical studies on the development of cancer concluded that anxiety, loss, and depression are strong predisposing influences, and that these emotions can cause a loss of vitality and weaken one's ability to resist disease. Many subsequent studies reached much the same conclusion.

In the 1920s, psychologist Elida Evans collected information on one hundred cancer patients and found that many of them had lost an important emotional relationship shortly before the onset of their illness. They seemed to have become so involved with one person, vocation, or cause that they neglected the development of their own individuality. When that person or relationship was removed, they felt cut off and found few internal resources for coping with the attendant stress. The literature indicates that the presence of cancer could be a sign of despair, and that this is often accompanied by feelings that there is no solution to one's problems.

More recent studies have corroborated these findings. Psychologist Lawrence LeShan studied and evaluated the emotional life histories of 450 cancer patients. He identified typical components in their life-history patterns.

> The first part involves a childhood or adolescence marked by feelings of isolation. There is a sense that intense and meaningful relationships are dangerous and bring pain and rejection. The second part of the pattern is centered upon the period during which a meaningful relationship is discovered, allowing the individual to enjoy a sense of acceptance by others and to find a meaning in his life. The third aspect of the pattern comes to the fore when the loss of that

central relationship occurs. Now there is a sense of utter despair, connected to but going beyond the childhood sense of isolation. In this third phase, the connection that life holds no more hope becomes paramount, and sometimes after the onset of the third phase, the first symptoms of cancer are noted.

The individuals participating in the above-mentioned study were described as "bottled up," unable to vent their feelings, to let others know when they felt hurt or angry. The "goodness" or "saintliness" of these people was a deceptively benign quality, actually a sign of their failure to believe in themselves sufficiently and indicative of their lack of hope. This basic emotional history prevailed in 76 percent of the cancer patients studied. Among the noncancer patients, this pattern was found among only 10 percent.

This personality configuration for the individual with cancer has been confirmed time and again. In 1940 a thirty-year longitudinal study was begun by Dr. Caroline Thomas, a psychologist at Johns Hopkins University, with the aim of identifying disease-related personality characteristics in individuals prior to any sign of disease. Since then, more than thirteen hundred students have been interviewed and their life history of illness followed. Those students who eventually developed cancer experienced a lack of closeness with their parents and rarely expressed strong feelings; these same individuals had a most distinctive personality profile, which included repression, loneliness, and hopelessness, a profile even more distinctive than those students who later committed suicide.

Other studies, conducted by Doctors A.H. Schmale and H. Iker in 1971, indicated that cancer patients tend to feel hopeless and helpless before the onset of disease. For these studies, questionable Pap smears were gathered together from a group of fifty-one women who were healthy but considered biologically predisposed to cancer of the cervix. Through tests and interviews a "helplessness-prone personality" was identified and used to predict which of these women would develop cancer. The predictions were 74 percent accurate.

Still another set of researchers, interested in the differences between patients with rapidly growing cancers and those with slow-growing cancers, found that they could with surprising accuracy predict from interviews alone how well their patients would do; their predictions correlated highly with the course of the disease. Those patients who were defensive and very anxious had fast-growing tumors. The individuals in the group with slow-growing tumors were more open and involved themselves more often in physical activity, thus reducing tension.

The powerful impact of the observed connection between psychological factors and tumor growth rate would seem to predict a drastic change in cancer management, yet the medical management of cancer and of most other diseases has not yet changed to any great degree.

The above examples give a composite picture of the type of personality that is prone to one particular disease—cancer. However, this profile offers information that is relevant to an exploration of psychological factors as they relate to any disease. Loss experienced preceding the diagnosis, inability to express feelings and emotions, feelings of isolation, helplessness, and despair—most people will recognize some aspect of themselves within this description, having at one time or another confronted death or separation, seemingly inexpressible feelings or insoluble dilemmas. These are all part of the struggle inherent in living, but just because one has these experiences does not mean that one has to go down a one-way street to illness. One has choices: the choice of inaction or constructive action.

To those of you who have recently been diagnosed with an illness, I recommend that you do not waste time blaming yourselves, feeling guilty, or becoming discouraged. Rather, examine and try to accept any responsibility you may feel for getting sick, and, at the same time, investigate ways to get better, using this information to stimulate your desire to get well. Your do not have to be a victim of your past nor of your personality: both personality and behavior can be changed. I have experienced this kind of transformation within myself and have observed it in many of my clients.

My advice to my clients is to work hand in hand with the medical profession: an accurate clinical diagnosis is needed before patients can make wise and informed decisions concerning their health. I suggest they listen carefully to their doctor's diagnosis and recommended treatment, obtain second and third opinions, and select the doctor with whom they feel the most comfortable and best able to communicate. I also suggest that they read extensively on the subject of their illness, that they take the time to consider various alternative types of treatment available to them, and that they then reach their own decision about what feels right to them. I want them to think carefully about how much responsibility they are prepared to take for their healing and how much medical help they feel they need. Their own belief in their treatment, whether it is self-healing or medical, seems to be the crucial factor.

When we emerge from a doctor's office, frightened and shocked, we are often completely unaware that there are alternatives to what the doctor has said. Unwittingly, and in trepidation, we sometimes make the doctor into a supreme being, with the divine right to decide what is best for us. Doctors themselves often encourage a "you're sick and I have the answer for you" relationship. The unfortunate outcome of this misplaced power is that if medical treatment does not produce the desired result, the doctor is blamed. I urge my clients to think for themselves. We all find this difficult at times, especially when it involves medical treatment. Most of us find it difficult to question authority, especially male authority. Some doctors use this attitude to their advantage to impose their will on patients. Dr. Robert Mendelsohn coined the word "mal(e)practice" to describe this phenomenon. The problem is serious but fortunately not insurmountable. We all must learn to make our own decisions regarding medical treatment.

Your health belongs to you. This idea is not new, but it is easier for some to accept than for others. Many excellent books have been written on this and related topics—in particular the limitations of the medical profession: Ivan Illich's *Medical Nemesis*, Thomas McKeown's *The Role of Medicine*, René Dubos's *Mirage of Health*, Robert Mendelsohn's *Confessions of a Medical Heretic*, and Dennis Jaffe's *Healing from Within*, to name a few.

Ivan Illich, the world-famous founder of the Center for Intercultural Documentation (CIDOC) in Cuernavaca, Mexico, is a provocative and profoundly humanistic writer who has persistently questioned the sanctity of the major institutions of our society. He has encouraged individuals to not submit themselves passively to them but to take responsibility for their own learning and health—to reclaim their autonomy as human beings. In *Medical Nemesis*, he offers a critique not just of the medical profession as a manipulative industry but of ourselves as its passive, slavish consumers. In *The Role of Medicine*, Dr. McKeown, professor emeritus of Social Medicine at the University of Birmingham, England, demonstrates that medical intervention has—as opposed to what is commonly assumed—historically had a relatively minor impact on levels of illness and disease and that social and environmental factors have been of far greater significance. Like Illich, he believes that it is the individual's right to control his or her own health; however, unlike Illich, who believes medicine creates more illness than it cures and proposes a dismantling of the entire industry, McKeown sees a continuing role for medicine in the promotion and development of health.

With his beautifully written *Mirage of Health*, published in 1959, renowned bacteriologist René Dubos fired one of the first salvos in the assault on modern man's complacent view of medical science as holding the potential to uncover a panacea for all our ills. This book surveys mankind's pursuit of health from ancient times to the present and shows that the "miracles" of modern medicine are largely illusionary. Twenty years later, Robert Mendelsohn, himself a doctor, continued the dialectic with his *Confessions of a Medical Heretic*. In this book, Mendelsohn offers a compelling, albeit somewhat one-sided, attack on modern medicine. Providing many shocking examples, he argues that most medical treatments given today are unnecessary, ineffective, and often dangerous and proposes that, in unquestioningly accepting the mystique of medicine, we have unwittingly allowed the medical profession to attain virtually the status of a priesthood.

Finally, in *Healing from Within*, psychologist Dennis Jaffe offers a comprehensive exploration of the psychological factors involved in both illness and recovery. He stresses that individuals are responsible in large part for activating and sustaining good health and suggests methods for accomplishing this goal.

While most would agree that the medical profession offers invaluable assistance in the areas of technology, clinical treatment, and support services, it is important to realize that doctors do not have all the answers, and that it is unreasonable and unrealistic to expect that they ever will. While physicians can assist the individual in becoming healthy, health itself is the intrinsic responsibility of each person. We each possess physiological, emotional, mental, and spiritual capacities that we can bring to the process of healing. We can mobilize these resources in conjunction with the help of the medical profession, choose to heal ourselves with alternative methods, or we can use the benefits of both. We each must discover our own personal journey to health.

☐ MYSTERY IN MEDICINE

The technology of modern medicine has established highly sophisticated surgical techniques and impressive physiological therapies. Powerful and successful though technology may be, when applied to human beings, it is simply not enough. In fact, medical technology is creating the misconception that contemporary medicine is extremely effective. Certainly, immunization has been effective with paralytic poliomyelitis, and vaccines have contributed to the decline of whooping cough and measles, but for most other infections, medicine can show no comparable results. Medical intervention to prevent death and lengthen life in the past three centuries has been less important than other influences. With the possible exception of diphtheria, mortality from common infections (tuberculosis, pneumonia, scarlet fever, pertussis) had already declined to quite a low level before effective immunization and antibiotics became available. Control of infection resulted mainly from modification of the depressed socio-economic conditions under which the infections occurred. The incidence of death from infectious diseases, for the most part, was essentially independent of medical intervention. Analysis of disease trends indicates that the environment is the primary determinant of the state of general health of any population.

Your own immune system, if you follow an adequate diet, is the most effective "vaccine" against most diarrheal, respiratory, and other common infections. Most noncommunicable diseases—cancer, for example—are more likely to be controlled by discovering and removing their causes than by intervention. Although treatment of most skin cancers has been effective, as has the diagnostic value of the Pap smear, we have little proof of effective treatment of most other cancers. The five-year survival rate in breast cancer cases is 50 percent, regardless of the frequency of medical checkups or the treatment used. No evidence exists that this rate differs from that of untreated women.

Until recently it was accepted without question that modern improvement in health resulted essentially from medical intervention, but it is often less effective than most people, including many doctors, believe. Doctors have a tendency to overestimate their effectiveness and underrate the risk of treatment and the prescription of drugs. It is understandably not easy for them or us to accept that medicine is not the major determinant of health.

Robert Mendelsohn points out that we must be aware of the doctors' self-interests. They do get more reward and recognition for *intervening* than for not intervening. Doctors are trained to intervene and *do* something rather than observe, wait, and take the chance that patients will get better all by themselves.

☐ IATROGENESIS

The technical term for doctor-made disease is iatrogenesis. It is composed of the Greek word for "physician" (iatros) and for "origin" (genesis). Iatrogenic disease comprises only illness that occurs as a result of professionally recommended treatment. An expanding proportion of the new burden of disease of the past twenty-five years is itself the result of medical intervention on behalf of those who are or might become sick.

The average frequency of reported accidents in hospitals is higher than in all industries except mines and high-rise building construction. A national survey indicates that accidents were the major cause of death in children in the United States—and that these accidents occurred more often in hospitals than in any other place. One in fifty children admitted to hospital suffered an accident while there that required specific treatment. The research on university or teaching hospitals is even more discouraging. It has been established that one out of every five patients admitted to a typical research hospital acquires an iatrogenic disease, sometimes trivial, usually requiring special treatment, and that one case in thirty leads to death. Half of these incidents result from complications in drug therapy, and one in ten comes from diagnostic procedures. Illich points out sardonically that, despite good intentions and claims to public service, with a similar record of performance a military officer would be relieved of his command and a restaurant or amusement center would be closed by the health or police department.

Illich warns us that disabling nondiseases result from the medical treatment of nonexistent diseases and are on the increase. That is why it is so imperative that each of us assumes more responsibility;

that we get second and third opinions from doctors; that we read about side effects of medications before taking them; that we try alternative nonmedical healing modalities.

☐ DRUGS

Throughout history, drugs, in whatever form, have been the badge of healing power. In ancient times, healing compounds were made from natural herbs and mysterious liquids. The physicians of today prescribe drugs made in chemical laboratories, yet these drugs are no less mysterious. Patients are rarely told what is in the drug or how it works.

> Medicines have always been potentially poisonous, but their unwanted side effects have increased with their power and widespread use. Every 24 to 36 hours, from 50% to 80% of adults in the U.S. and the U.K. swallow a medically prescribed chemical. Some take the wrong drug; others get an old or contaminated batch, and others a counterfeit; others take several drugs in dangerous combinations; and still others receive injections with improperly sterilized syringes. (Illich, *Limits of Medicine*)

Drugs are now being so overprescribed that they are causing more illness in the form of side effects than they are curing. DES is a case in point.

DES is a synthetic form of estrogen that was prescribed for three to six million women in the United States between 1941 and 1971. DES stands for the chemical name diethylstilbestrol but has been manufactured under more than two hundred brand names and given out throughout the United States and in many other parts of the world in the form of pills, injections, and suppositories.

Despite studies as early as the 1930s indicating that estrogens were carcinogenic in laboratory animals, the Federal Drug Administration (FDA) approved DES in 1942 for lactation suppression, treatment of menopausal symptoms, and vaginitis. In 1947, the FDA extended approval of DES in even higher doses for use during pregnancy, even though there had been no studies to examine potential effects on the fetus or the pregnant women. Doctors commonly prescribed DES if a woman had a history of miscarriage, diabetes, high blood pressure, or slight bleeding during pregnancy.

Although studies showed conclusively as early as 1953 that DES was ineffective in preventing miscarriage, the FDA did not warn against using it in pregnancy until 1971, after its link to cancer was firmly established. During the intervening eighteen years, millions were needlessly exposed.

In 1977, the University of Chicago was sued for $77 million by more than a thousand women who unwittingly took part in an experiment there using DES thirty years earlier. Many of the daughters of the women who had taken DES were developing vaginal cancer, and the male offspring of these women had a significantly high rate of genital malformation. Some of the women themselves were dying of cancer.

Even so, DES is sometimes still prescribed for menopausal problems, for lactation suppression, for morning-after contraception, for acne, and in advanced cases of breast cancer.

Most of us have blindly trusted antibiotics. Antibiotics work almost exclusively against bacterial infections and are powerless against viral conditions such as the common cold and flu. They do not shorten the course of these ailments, do not prevent complications, and do not reduce the number of pathogenic organisms in your nose or throat. They can, however, cause skin rash, vomiting, diarrhea, and fever. Even so, each year 95 percent of Americans will go to the doctor with a cold and come away with a prescription—half of which will be for antibiotics. They will pay for something that is not effective and will be exposed to the risks of side effects.

Tetracycline became so popular in office practices and outpatient clinics that it was known as the "house call" antibiotic. It has, however, been found responsible for thousands of children having yellow-green teeth and tetracycline deposits in their bones.

More impotence is caused by drug therapy than by psychological problems.

> In the United States, the volume of the drug business has grown by a factor of 100 during the current century: 20,000 tons of aspirin are consumed per year, almost 225 tablets per person ... central-nervous-system agents are the fastest-growing sector of the pharmaceutical market, now making up 31 per cent of total sales. Dependence on tranquillizers has risen by 290 per cent since 1962, a period during which the per capita consumption of liquor rose by only 23 per cent and the estimated consumption of illegal opiates by about 50 per cent. (Illich, *Limits of Medicine*, pp. 78-9)

Valium is the number-one prescription drug, accounting for over $130 million in sales in 1979 in the United States. Not only is the drug addictive: the indications for the prescription of Valium and the side effects are identical! These include anxiety, fatigue, depression, muscle spasms, and agitation.

It is imperative that you obtain pertinent information regarding any prescription, including potential side effects. You can find lists of precautions and adverse reactions to drugs in the *Compendium of Pharmaceuticals and Specialities*. In the United States similar information is available in the *Physicians' Desk Reference*. These are available in almost every public library and are written in such a manner that you will be able to understand what you need to know.

You can also ask your druggist or doctor to inform you completely of all side effects before taking any medication. Compare these effects with what you are already experiencing.

☐ RADIATION

Beware the X ray machine. It could be the most hazardous piece of equipment in the doctor's office and the hospital. So-called "absolutely harmless" radiation has resulted in a plethora of thyroid tumors.

> Thyroid lesions, many of them cancerous, are now turning up by the thousands in people who were exposed to head, neck, and upper chest radiation twenty to thirty years ago. Thyroid cancer can develop after an amount of radiation that is less than that produced by ten bite-wing dental x-rays. Scientists . . . have implicated x-rays in the development of diabetes, cardiovascular disease, stroke, high blood pressure, and cataracts—all associated with aging. Other studies have matched radiation to cancer, blood disorders, and tumors of the central nervous system. Conservative estimates peg the number of deaths each year directly attributable to medical and dental radiation at 4,000. (Mendelsohn, *Confessions of a Medical Heretic*, p. 27)

There is well-published scientific documentation showing that mammography itself (breast X rays) may cause more breast cancer than it will detect! Even so, hundreds of thousands of women are still having breast X rays. Think, read, discuss, and make your own decision before submitting your breasts to radiation. (Bailar, 1976)

☐ DIAGNOSTIC PROCEDURE AND LABORATORY TESTING

Diagnostic proceedings are often misleading or harmful. A recent study showed that physicians supposedly trained to interpret mammograms were no more accurate than untrained physicians in spotting breast cancer on mammograms. Medical testing laboratories can be extremely inaccurate.

> In 1975, the Center for Disease Control (CDC) reported that its surveys of labs across the country demonstrated that ten to forty per cent of their work in bacteriological testing was unsatisfactory, thirty to fifty per cent failed various simple clinical chemistry tests, twelve to eighteen per cent flubbed blood grouping and typing, and twenty to thirty percent botched hemoglobin and serum electrolyte tests. Overall, erroneous results were obtained in more than a quarter of all the tests. (Mendelsohn, p. 29.)

These results indicate the best tests by the best labs. Most of us believe that medical research workers have made a supreme contribution to the saving of human life. We note the decline of infections and trust that tomorrow a cure for cancer and a utopian solution to mental illness will be found. We are reminded, however, that the contribution of laboratory science has virtually come to an end, and that almost no modern basic research in the medical sciences has any direct bearing on the prevention of disease or on the improvement of medical care.

How many millions of dollars have medical researchers spent in their quest for a cure for the common cold? And we still drink lots of fluids, get a little rest, and wait for the body to heal itself.

If you are as shocked as I was by some of the above opinions and facts, I suggest that you do a little more reading. There is no doubt that the discovery of micro-organisms in the laboratory helped to control the *origins* of infectious diseases. The infections themselves, however, declined largely because of the removal of the ill effects of poverty. The noncommunicable diseases that have replaced the infections are evidently not responsive to the same changes; otherwise they would not be there.

☐ SURGERY

Coronary bypass surgery was thought to be the answer to the soaring rate of death by heart attack in the United States.

> A seven-year study by the Veterans' Administration of more than a thousand people found that except for high-risk patients with rare left-main artery disease, the coronary bypass provided no benefit. (Mendelsohn, p. 101)

> In another unusual study ... one group underwent the complete operation, while the other group members were cut open and sewn back up. Both groups were informed they had received the entire surgery. Follow-up studies indicated that all patients fared equally well in postoperative evaluations of their symptoms. (Beecher, "The Powerful Placebo")

There are approximately one million hysterectomies performed every year in the United States—the highest rate for any operation. Apparently many of them are unnecessary. In six New York hospitals studied, 43 percent of the hysterectomies reviewed were found to be unjustified. Women with abnormal bleeding from the uterus and abnormally heavy menstrual blood flow were given hysterectomies even though other treatments—or no treatment at all—would likely have worked just as well. "In prepaid group practices where surgeons are paid a steady salary not tied to how many operations they perform, hysterectomies and tonsillectomies occur only about one-third as often as in fee-for-service situations" (Mendelsohn, p. 105).

Surgery for cancer can often cause more harm than benefit. After the skin is cut open, the spread of tumor cells can be observed in the peripheral blood.

But the knife cuts on.

Discuss recommended surgery with different doctors in different medical or environmental settings before making your decision.

☐ DEATHBED TECHNOLOGY

If you are unfortunate enough to have sick, elderly relatives admitted to hospital, you may be surprised and horrified by the lack of humanity in dealing with them. Your relative will probably be immediately taken over by the technological machinery of the hospital. The $500-a-day deathbeds will have all the latest electronic gear. Diagnosis and treatment become paramount; discussion of causes or influences that could be modified or removed are avoided. Staff will treat your elderly but will generally not care what they are feeling, nor pay heed to any entreaty, such as a request to die in a peaceful home environment. The patients will probably be examined, incised, stitched, drugged, suctioned, catheterized, probed, and even pummeled by so many interns who don't know them but do this in the name of research. The doctors will consult as they stand over your kin and discuss this precious person as if he or she were an inanimate object. Rarely will one of the staff find the time to hold this person's hand, to make eye contact, to ask what is needed, or to find out how your relative is feeling emotionally or spiritually. These people are likely to pick up an infection because of their treatment and die from a cause of which you will never be informed. The last sounds your relative will hear will be the electronic whistle on the cardiogram. You will finally be allowed to participate by paying the bill.

Doctors devote an inordinate amount of time to death-oriented activities. This becomes particularly evident during a doctors' strike. In 1976 in Bogotá, Colombia, there was a fifty-two-day period during which the doctors supplied only emergency care. The *National Catholic Reporter* described "a string of unusual side effects" from the strike. The death rate went down 35 percent.

> An 18 percent drop in the death rate occurred in Los Angeles County in 1976 when doctors there went on strike to protest soaring malpractice insurance premiums. Dr. Milton Roemer, a professor of health care administration at UCLA, surveyed seventeen major hospitals and found that 60 fewer operations were performed. When the strike ended, the death rate went right back up to where it had been before the strike. (Mendelsohn, p. 186)

The same thing happened in Israel in 1973 when the doctors reduced their daily patient contact from sixty-five thousand to seven thousand. The strike lasted a month. According to the Jerusalem Burial Society, the Israeli death rate dropped 50 percent during that month. There had not been such a profound decrease in mortality since the last doctors' strike twenty years earlier!

The treatment of disease by modern medicine is often ineffective, and treatment may often be more dangerous to health than the disease for which it was designed.

☐ MEDICAL NEMESIS

Ambrosia, in mythology, is the divine potion that made the gods immortal. Ivan Illich suggests that we humans have become addicted to ambrosia in the form of unlimited so-called medical improvements in health. Medical professionals generally are disciples of Asclepius, the first physician according to Greek legend, who achieved fame not by teaching wisdom but by mastering the use of the knife. They are also peddlers of ambrosia, and the result of dependence on ambrosia is "Medical Nemesis." For the Greeks, nemesis was the inevitable punishment for attempting to be a hero rather than a human being. And we have encouraged physicians by insisting on their heroism rather than on their humanity.

> Medical Nemesis is more than all clinical iatrogeneses put together, more than the sum of malpractice, negligence, professional callousness, political maldistribution, medically decreed disability and all the consequences of medical trial and error. *It is the expropriation of man's coping ability* by a maintenance system which keeps him geared up at the service of the industrial system. (Illich, p. 160) [Emphasis mine]

Our collective refusal to face nemesis results in our abetting a system that first denies our autonomy (the right to make our own decisions with regard to our bodies and our health), and, second, promotes an industry engineered by sociopolitical constructs, "Industrial Nemesis." The reversal of nemesis can come only from within ourselves by recovering the will to care for ourselves and by working to obtain the recognition of this right legally, politically, and institutionally.

☐ PERSONAL BEHAVIOR

If you take a world view of health, you will probably find that the order of importance of the chief influences on health is close to what it has been in the past: nutritional, environmental, behavioral, and clinical.

The balance, however, between diseases associated with poverty and those associated with affluence is changing. Diseases associated with affluence are related to comparatively recent behavioral changes: for example, consumption of refined foods, sedentary living resulting mainly from extensive use of the car, and cigarette smoking on a significant scale. Smoking causes eight in every ten cases of lung cancer. Although it is difficult to estimate accurately the relative importance of behavioral and other influences, it is possible to assess the ill effects of smoking.

In the past century the improvement in the life expectancy of mature males *from all causes* has been reduced by at least half by smoking alone. Because so large a reduction was due to a single practice, we can conclude that in advanced countries such as ours our behavior is now more important than any other influence on health. Many of these changes in behavior are characteristic of an affluent society. It would seem, then, that diseases associated with affluence are now more predominant. Clearly, we should be spending less time and money in the laboratories and more time investigating the effects of personality and behavioral change on illness and health.

Since 1950 the age-adjusted death rate from cancer of all kinds has risen from 170 to 185 per 100,000 population in the United States. This was reported in the prestigious *New England Journal of Medicine* (Spring 1986), with the conclusion that *prevention is the main hope* of lowering the death rate. The statistics for Canada are similar.

Another report from the same journal concluded that we are losing the war against cancer, with the odds of dying from the disease increasing in the past three decades. This study, by Doctors John Bailar of the Harvard School of Public Health and Elaine Smith of the University of Iowa Medical Center, recommends that scientists concentrate on finding ways to prevent cancer, *not new ways to treat it.* They state, "There is no reason to think that, on the whole, cancer is becoming any less common."

Personal behavior is now more meaningful and of more consequence to our well-being than either malnutrition or environmental risk. This emphasizes the importance of lifestyle change, so that we may stop the current epidemic of cancer and other diseases of our time.

It is imperative that we assume responsibility and face the role that our own behavior plays in our health. The rest of this book is devoted to helping you discover just what you can do to increase the quality of your health, the steps you can take to reclaim responsibility for what is rightly yours—your health.

13

DEMYSTIFYING HEALING

There is no question that the "set of the spirit" can alter—even arrest for significant periods of time—the course of life-threatening disease.—Emerson Day, President, New York Academy of Science

Those of you who have an illness and decide to change your life history pattern need to recognize three important belief systems. The first is your own. Your beliefs about your disease, treatment, doctor, and self are crucial influential factors in the journey toward health or disease during and after treatment. Next is the belief system of your family and friends, those people whose reaction to illness may be meaningful. Educating family and friends and helping them to change their beliefs about disease are vitally important in influencing the direction of your illness. Third, you should find out the perspective of your physician on healing. In contradiction to objective scientific experimental results, the all too common belief among doctors is that disease comes from outside the individual, that they are the authorities, and that the individual has little or nothing to do with his or her recovery.

☐ THE SIGNIFICANCE OF ATTITUDES AND BELIEFS

Twenty years ago psychologist R. Rosenthall conducted experiments demonstrating that altered expectancies resulting in unconscious changes in behavior can produce dramatic changes in outcome— and can work both positively and negatively. Two of his studies illustrate how attitudes and beliefs can become self-fulfilling prophecies. In the first, graduate students conducting animal research were told that certain rats were exceptionally bright and would complete a maze more rapidly than other rats that were dull and would do poorly. Actually, all the rats were equally clever; there was no measurable difference in prior performance time or intelligence. The results of this experiment, however, indicated that the supposedly bright rats performed substantially better than the so-called dull rats. A positive belief or expectancy of behavior was somehow communicated from teacher to student to rat.

In the second study, a number of elementary-school children were divided into two similar groups according to IQ, academic grades, gender, and ethnic background. Their teachers were told that the students in one group were very bright and that those in the other group were of only average intelligence. When tested eight months later, the children in the so-called "bright" group had dramatically raised their IQ levels over those of the children in the other group. The only difference between the two groups was the expectation created in the teachers' minds.

Oncologist Carl Simonton has confirmed the effects of positive expectancy in a study of 152 cancer patients at Travis Air Force Base, the major air force medical facility on the West Coast. In this study, each patient was rated on his or her attitude toward treatment. Those patients who had been assessed as having positive attitudes responded better to treatment over an eighteen-month period, regardless of the severity of their disease.

K. Pelletier, renowned author, clinical psychologist, and director of the Psychosomatic Medicine Center of Gladman Memorial Hospital, Berkeley, California, states the case as follows:

> Perhaps the most essential feature of holistic systems of healing is the profound alteration required in an individual's belief system. Once an individual adopts the concept that he is an *active and responsible participant in the process of self-healing*, he is no longer the passive recipient of a cure. In modern science, ranging from the neurophysiology of consciousness to quantum physics, it has become evident that the structure of personal belief systems concerning the nature of the self and the universe governs experiences .... *Inherent in any system of belief is a self-fulfilling prophesy*: what is expected is observed, and what is observed confirms the expectation .... One immediate implication of this principle is that when an individual alters his belief system, he becomes aware of vast new realms of possibility. Paradigms are subject to change, and the pressing need for a more comprehensive interpretation of man and his

universe is all around us: in the sorcery of Carlos Castaneda's Don Juan, in the metaphysical implications of quantum physics and consciousness research, and in the applications of meditation and biofeedback in the healing professions. [Emphases mine]

☐ THE PLACEBO EFFECT

The placebo effect, the effect of faith, involves another powerful process. The word placebo is Latin and means 'I shall please.' In medical terminology it refers to a pill or treatment given to humor, rather than to medicate, a patient. Yet the results are often quite startling and demonstrate the power that a belief system has over the self-restorative capacity of the body. The late Dr. Henry Beecher, noted anesthesiologist at Harvard University, who persisted for many years in the study of this phenomenon and reviewed studies of placebo treatments for dozens of ailments, found that 35 percent of over a hundred patients experienced satisfactory relief with placebos used instead of regular medication for a wide range of medical problems. More recent research suggests that such placebo-induced results are not simply the effects of the imagination but are the results of actual physical change, and medical scholars are at last beginning to search for a mechanism in the brain that could initiate physical change as a result of mental suggestion. Dr. Stewart Wolf, vice-president for medical affairs at St. Luke's Hospital in Bethlehem, Pennsylvania for example, has discovered that a placebo can produce abnormal numbers of a certain type of blood cell in the immune system, or reduce the amount of fat and protein in the blood. Twenty-five years ago Dr. A.K. Shapiro wrote in the *American Journal of Psychotherapy,* "Placebos can have profound effects on organic illness, including incurable malignancies."

A paper published in 1951 provides a singular example of this phenomenon:

> A case study is reported of a patient with far advanced lymphosarcoma who begged to be entered into a study of Krebiozen—a drug claimed to have cancer curative properties. Upon the initial administration of Krebiozen, his tumor masses "melted like snowballs on a hot stove," and having previously required an oxygen mask to breathe, he became fully active and flew his plane at 12,000 feet with no discomfort. When clinical reports appeared announcing the ineffectiveness of the drug, he returned to his bedridden state. His physician, then, in a last attempt to offer him life, told him not to believe what he had read about the drugs, informing him that the preparation deteriorated upon standing and that it would be given him at double strength. Actually the injection was water. The man again evidenced rapid remission. He continued to improve until it was announced in the press that the American Medical Association and the Food and Drug Administration had found Krebiozen to be a worthless preparation. The man died within a few days. (Achterberg, Simonton, and Matthews-Simonton, 1976)

One might suspect this case history of being apocryphal; nevertheless, it is not incompatible with the facts and well describes not only the immense power that belief can play in the course of disease, but also the perils of placing the responsibility for health outside oneself.

Gregory Bateson saw placebos as a way in which the mind-body can form alternative messages—as carriers of messages. Hence, a patient can *know* that what he or she is taking is a placebo and it can work *because* of this—because it is really just the form given to the message, which, in the case of the placebo, is the message to heal.

As he looked back at his own experience with cancer, Bateson was inclined to think that

> I handled the whole bloody business, from the very beginning to spitting blood, through to writing the book [*Mind and Nature: A Necessary Unity*], as a sort of enormous placebo of some kind, which I brought upon myself. I believe in mind and, therefore, in placebos. The doctors aren't crazy about placebos because they think they are deceitful. Because they themselves are committed to a materialism that dictates that salt pills should not work, they think they should never tell the patient they are giving him a salt pill. Therefore, if they tell the patient it's a salt pill, they are probably correct in saying that this would stop the effect of the salt pill, because in their voices would be the suggestion that it's not going to work because it's a salt pill.

Bateson believed that all this is a good deal of nonsense, and comes out of the materialistic stance to which doctors are committed and of which he did not approve. He stated that "physiological medicine, along with behavioral psychology and Darwinian evolution, does its best to exclude mind as an explanatory principle and the training of doctors turns them strongly towards this materialism."

Bateson did not agree that the pill would not work because a person believed it was a placebo—an opinion confirmed by recent experiments. He stated that the experimental evidence even then indicated that salt pills have about 30 percent effectiveness for many types of illnesses, compared to known effective drugs. This means that any drug is always operating with at least that 30 percent on its side. Even the most physiological drug is also a placebo; but of course doctors do not stress this point.

Bateson also pointed out that the most conspicuous techniques of healing by visualization, which are now being developed outside established medicine, invite the patient to invent his or her own placebo; this placebo cannot be a lie in such a case. He went on to say, "A major operation in which they take away a rib and fuck you up but good is quite a considerable placebo experience if you think about it as such."

The effect of the placebo proves that there is no real separation between mind and body. Health and illness are the result of the interaction. Norman Cousins, author, editor, and senior lecturer at the School of Medicine, University of California at Los Angeles, explains: "The placebo, then is an emissary between the will to live and the body. The placebo has a role to play in transforming the will to live from a poetical conception to a physical reality and a governing force."

☐ STRESS AND YOUR RESPONSE

Hans Selye defined stress as "the nonspecific response of the body to any demand." He discovered that stress causes certain changes in the structure and chemistry of the body, some of which are signs of damage, others of which are manifestations of the body's adaptive reactions—mechanisms of defense against stress. Selye named the totality of these changes "the stress syndrome," and described it as encompassing three stages: the alarm reaction, resistance, and exhaustion. The alarm reaction is the spontaneous response of the body to whatever is causing stress: the body readies itself for action and responds on an instinctive level with a fight or flight reaction, a movement toward or away from the stressor. Because neither of these reactions is particularly condoned in our society, and because we have not yet learned to manage stress satisfactorily, many individuals internalize the impulse to fight or flee, causing their bodies increasing tension.

The next stage is resistance. The nervous system and endocrine (hormonal) system play extremely important roles in maintaining resistance during stress. They help to maintain the structure and function of the body, despite exposure to stress-producing agents such as nervous tension, injection, or poison. The natural physiological process of the body toward a balanced and harmonious state is called homeostasis. Pain and illness are among the ways it calls for attention. The body attempts to communicate that something is out of rhythm and that some aspect of body-mind-spirit needs more attention or change. When my heart began to give me pain, it was (in hindsight) as if a friend was warning me, signaling that some aspect of my being was out of balance.

Without some form of intervention, a body under stress will enter the third stage: exhaustion, imbalance, disequilibrium, or disease (in my case, it could have been a heart attack). Selye asserted that all physical and emotional illness is a manifestation of adaptive reactions.

For example, he discovered that chronic stress frequently produces imbalances in the hormonal secretions that regulate body functions. He further discovered that *chronic stress suppresses the immune system* responsible for engulfing and destroying cancerous cells. When response to stress is not neutralized through physical activity or emotional expression, tissue destruction results. According to Seyle, the physical conditions that stress produces are similar to those under which an abnormal cell could reproduce or spread.

Selye's research has been supported by studies involving both laboratory animals and humans. It has been scientifically demonstrated that the intensity of cancerous growth in animals placed under stress is much higher than in nonstressed animals.

A telling study conducted by Dr. Vernon Riley in 1975 indicated that by varying stress levels the incidence of breast cancer in mice, all of which had a genetic predisposition to the disease, similarly can be seen to vary. Malignancy increased up to 90 percent under stressful conditions, while remaining at 7 percent in a protected environment. Although generalizations from animal research to human pathology are difficult, the implications from this study are extremely important; it links research in immunology with the findings of stress researchers: "The data further imply that once a cancer cell escapes to an organizational state beyond the limited defensive abilities of immunological surveillance, the production of a lethal tumor may then be inevitable and not reversible by natural host defenses."

It is general knowledge today that environmental factors influence tumor development and that the mechanisms responsible for this growth are hormonal imbalances, immune incompetence, and altered connective-tissue reactions. These mechanisms are influenced by the central nervous system mediated through hypothalamic regulation. The evidence is conclusive that prolonged or intense stress predisposes living organisms to the development of malignancy and significantly influences the course of disease.

Many of you have already observed from your own experience that illness is often likely to have been preceded by some major emotional upset or stressful event. A scale associating clusters of stressful events with illness and severity of illness was devised by Dr. Thomas Holmes of the University of Washington

TEST YOUR STRESS THRESHOLD

Tensions, pressures, the drive to succeed—even too many changes can add up to STRESS.

University of Michigan researchers found that a boring job is just as stressful, if not more so, than a harder one. Workers were the happiest when they had a challenging job and the skills and resources to do it. Scientists, for example, liked their jobs the most, and they also lived the longest.

The stress of losing a job is a well-recognized health hazard. The nations high unemployment rate already is being blamed for an increase in the rates of infant mortality, alcoholism, child abuse, as well as suicide.

A flood of studies have convincingly demonstrated that the more stress a person is exposed to as a result of life changes, the greater are his/her chances of getting sick.

The University of Washington's Holmes devised a scale of 43 life changes that could accurately predict a person's risk of becoming ill.

Death of a spouse was the most stressful event, rating 100 points. Among the top changes were divorce, 73; marital separation, 65; jail term, 63; death of close family member, 63; personal injury or illness, 53; marriage, 50; fired at work, 47; marital reconciliation, 45; and retirement, 45.

Even such desirable changes as a new job or a vacation produced stress on Holmes's danger list.

A person scoring less than 150 points had about one in three chances of a serious illness in the next two years. A score between 150 and 300 increased this risk to 50 per cent. If you scored over 300 points, your chances of becoming sick are almost 90 per cent, according to Holmes.

Some of the life changes, like the death of a spouse, cannot be avoided. Others can. By postponing marriage, college, a move, or other change to keep your score under 300 in a two-year period, Holmes said, you can reduce the chance of illness.

Score yourself on the life change test

If any of these events have happened to you in the last 12 months, please check Happened column and enter Value in Score column.

Item No.	Item Value	Happened (x)	Your Score	Life Event
1	100	___	___	Death of a Spouse
2	73	___	___	Divorce
3	65	___	___	Marital separation
4	63	___	___	Jail term
5	63	___	___	Death of a close family member
6	53	___	___	Personal injury or illness
7	50	___	___	Marriage
8	47	___	___	Fired at work
9	45	___	___	Marital reconciliation
10	45	___	___	Retirement
11	44	___	___	Change in health of family member
12	40	___	___	Pregnancy
13	39	___	___	Sex difficulties
14	39	___	___	Gain of new family member
15	39	___	___	Business readjustment
16	38	___	___	Change in financial state
17	37	___	___	Death of close friend
18	36	___	___	Change to different line of work
19	35	___	___	Change in number of arguments with spouse
20	31	___	___	Mortgage over $10,000
21	30	___	___	Foreclosure of mortgage or loan
22	29	___	___	Change in responsibilities at work
23	29	___	___	Son or daughter leaving home
24	29	___	___	Trouble with in-laws
25	28	___	___	Outstanding personal achievement
26	26	___	___	Spouse begins or stops work
27	26	___	___	Begin or end school
28	25	___	___	Change in living conditions
29	24	___	___	Revision of personal habits
30	23	___	___	Trouble with boss
31	20	___	___	Change in work hours or conditions
32	20	___	___	Change in residence
33	20	___	___	Change in schools
34	19	___	___	Change in recreation
35	19	___	___	Change in church activities
36	18	___	___	Change in social activities
37	17	___	___	Mortgage or loan less than $10,000
38	16	___	___	Change in sleeping habits
39	15	___	___	Change in number of family get-togethers
40	15	___	___	Change in eating habits
41	13	___	___	Vacation
42	12	___	___	Christmas
43	11	___	___	Minor violations of the law

Total score for 12 months ____

Note: The more change you have, the more likely you are to get sick. Of those people with over 300 for the past year, almost 80 percent get sick in the near future; with 150 to 299 about 50 per cent get sick in the near future; with less than 150, only about 30 per cent get sick in the near future.

School of Medicine and his associate Dr. R. Rahe. They assigned numerical values to forty-three common life changes, with the relative adaptive demands of each registered on a scale from 1 to 100. The sorts of changes represented in this scheme are events such as birth, marriage, death, change of address, and change of job, and the total of the numerical values of the stressful events one has been or is experiencing indicates the degree of stress with which one is living.

Holmes's and Rahe's rating scale is printed above. Try applying the scale to yourself. If the value given to a specific event does not feel right for you, substitute your own value for the event. It has been found that with this scale illness can be predicted with great accuracy. The scale has been used on over five thousand subjects: those who suffered stress-related disorders such as tuberculosis, heart disease, cancer, multiple sclerosis, skin disease, and mental illness experienced significantly high scores in the year preceding the onset of illness. For example, 37 percent of those who scored between 150 and 200 in a twelve-month period contracted a serious ailment during that year. Those with scores between 200 to 300 had over a 50 percent chance of becoming sick; 80 percent of those with scores over 300 experienced illness within the year. A correlation was also found between the severity of the illness and the elevation of the score, especially in relation to chronic, stress-related illnesses. It appears that the more critical a life change is, whether it is joyful or sad, the greater the effort that is expended in adapting to it. This effort may lower resistance to disease. It is also clear that if you do not discharge the physiological response to stress, tension builds up in the body. Chronic stress can decrease resistance to disease and play a strong role in illness.

The scale does not, however, predict reaction to

stress. How you manage or cope with stress is even more significant than the level of stress you are exposed to. In another study, 51 percent of the people with scores of over 300 did *not* get sick. In my experience of individuals under stress, I have found that the meaning or significance they attach to the stressful event can be decisive, as can the attitude they develop following the stressful event.

☐ A PSYCHOPHYSIOLOGICAL GUIDE

Some of my clients have been diagnosed as "medically incurable" by their doctors—according to national cancer statistics, they faced an average life expectancy of one year. When individuals believe that only the medical profession can help them, and when their doctors then tell them that they can no longer offer any help and that they probably have only a few months to live, they naturally feel hopeless, trapped, and helpless and usually fulfill their doctors' expectations. This can be changed.

Stephanie Matthews-Simonton and Carl Simonton have developed a hypothetical "mind/body" guide showing how psychological and physical states work together and describe how a stressful event or condition produces an emotional response. Emotional events are correlated with activity in the part of the brain known as the limbic lobe, or visceral brain. The limbic system records stress and its effect, as well as all other feelings and sensations. The hypothalamus, another small area in the brain, is the major pathway by which the limbic system influences the body. It is also a control center for major regulatory functions, including the immune system.

A MIND/BODY MODEL OF CANCER DEVELOPMENT

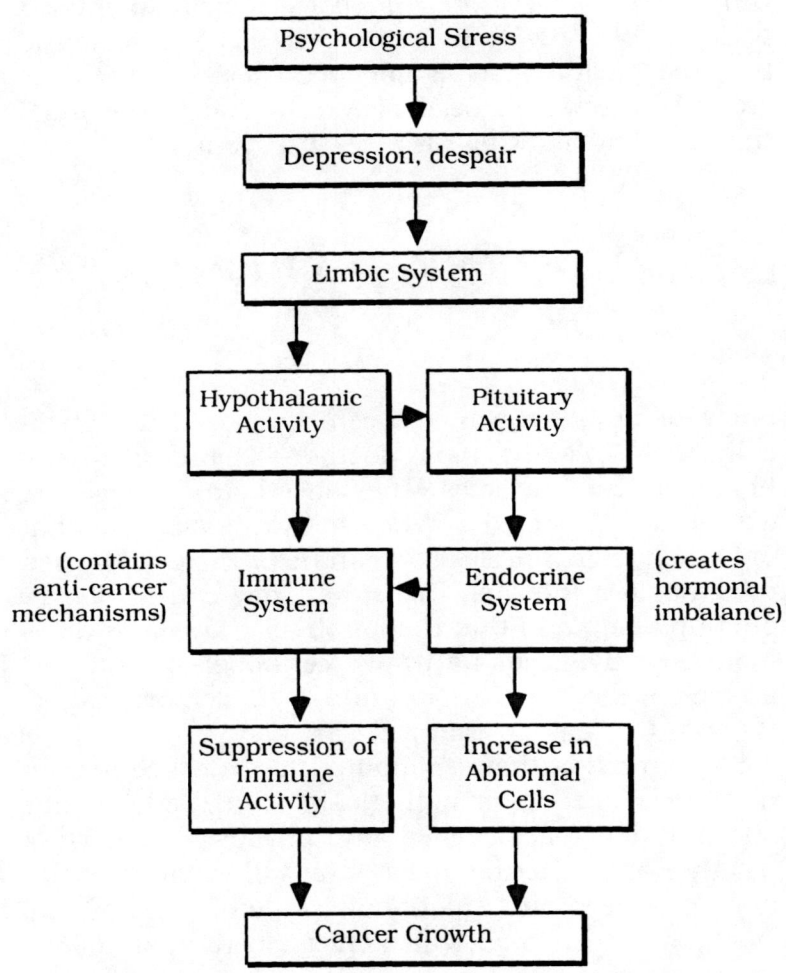

Simonton, O. Carl, S. Matthews-Simonton, and J. Creighton, *Getting Well Again* (Bantam Books, 1980).

A MIND/BODY MODEL OF RECOVERY

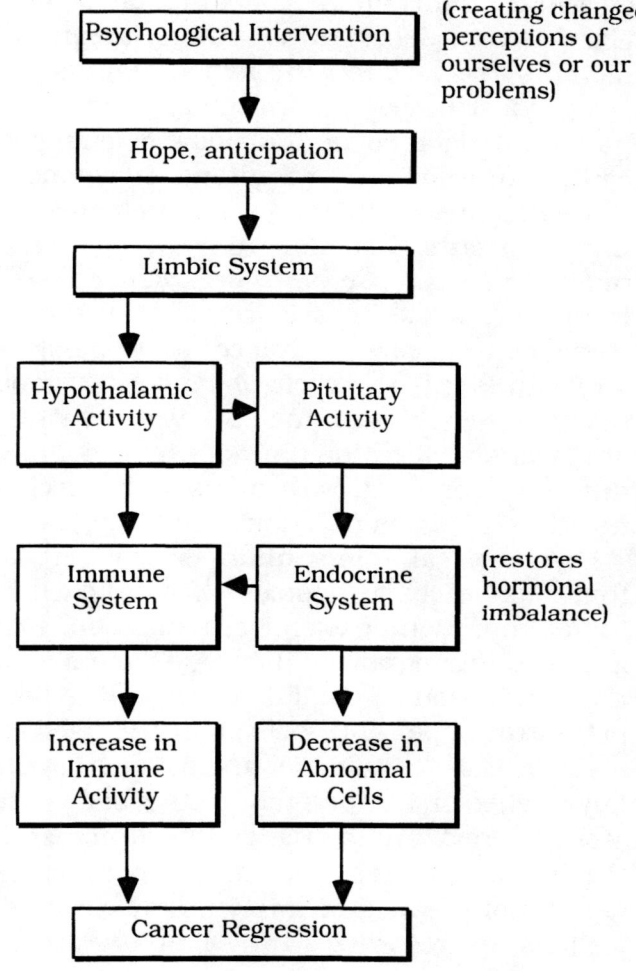

Simonton, O. Carl, S. Matthews-Simonton, and J. Creighton, *Getting Well Again* (Bantam Books, 1980).

When various types of activity take place in the hypothalamus, the pituitary gland—the body's master gland—receives messages via both neural and chemical connections. The function of the pituitary gland is best described as one of integrating all hormonal activity. When the hypothalamus responds to stress, it triggers the pituitary gland so that the hormonal balance of the body is changed. Significantly, an imbalance in adrenal hormones indicates a greater susceptibility to carcinogenic substances. Cancer occurs then not from a single causal factor but from a decrease in an organism's resistance and from an increase in abnormal cell production. Both these factors can be traced to the psychologically stressful event. The cycle of cancer development can, however, be reversed; the pathways by which feelings are translated into physiological conditions conducive to cancer growth can also be used to restore health. The tool is psychological intervention.

Psychological intervention is any regular activity that encourages self-esteem. This might be a satisfying hobby, regular exercise, relaxation, journal writing, meditation, psychotherapy—virtually any activity that gives you satisfaction. Feeling good gives impetus to hope and belief in the effectiveness of activity or of specific treatment, such as psychotherapy. Belief in the potency of the body's defenses is strengthened, and a change in self-perception and in the ability to cope effectively occurs; feelings of depression, fear, and anxiety may decrease. Altered feelings are recorded in the limbic system and positive messages are sent to the hypothalamus, which helps in the re-establishment of the body's equilibrium. The hypothalamus reverses the suppression of the immune system so that the body's defenses once again mobilize against abnormal cells. The pituitary gland sends messages to the rest of the endocrine system, restoring the body's hormonal balance. With immune activity, the production of abnormal cells decreases, resulting in regression of the disease: "Statistically, the results are inconclusive, but the Simonton team is averaging approximately 20 to 30 percent higher rates of remission or cure than traditional medical treatment records can demonstrate, and an even higher figure applies when compared to known instances of spontaneous remission" (Robinson, 1976).

The following is a comparison compiled by the Simontons of the survival times of cancer patients receiving, under their care, medical treatment and psychotherapy and the U.S. medical national survival time for individuals with similar cancers.

COMPARISON OF SURVIVAL TIMES

TYPE OF CANCER PATIENTS	MEDICAL NATIONAL SURVIVAL TIME (Months)	OBSERVED MEDIAN SURVIVAL TIME OF SIMONTON'S PATIENTS (Months)
Breast	16	35
Bowel	11	21
Lung	6	14

The Simontons discovered three outstanding differences between those who die and those who go on living: the latter have a different attitude toward disease, they have a positive outlook on life, and they believe they can exert some force on, or influence the course of their disease. I have found these differences confirmed in my research for this book and with my own clients.

YOUR BODY AS METAPHOR AND FRIEND

Our bodies work on our behalf. They are amazing vessels in which we are privileged to reside. Our remarkable immune system—the body's natural defense—is designed to protect us from disease and to contain or destroy any renegade cells. Current medical thinking suggests that all of us produce cancer cells in our bodies from time to time, either in response to externally originating agents such as radiation or synthetic compounds or simply due to inaccurate cellular reproduction. This concept suggests that cancer cells develop frequently but rarely progress into clinical malignancy because the body's defense mechanisms destroy them before they can take hold.

The body has a remarkably ally: its system of surveillance. Normally, the body's immune system keeps close watch for any abnormal cells and destroys them, hence the term "surveillance." Cancer can be compared to tuberculosis, polio, or the common cold in that many people may be exposed to it but few develop it. Consequently, for cancer (as well as other illnesses) to occur, the immune system, the body's system of surveillance, must be inhibited in some way. Emotional stress reactions are major factors in creating immunological deficiencies.

It is essential that we all learn to recognize the body's messages. Sam Keen, psychologist and author of *The Myths We Live and Die By*, describes three distinct stages that you may encounter when experiencing disease. The first stage is the "I/It" stage, in which you believe yourself to be a victim of external factors, such as germs, or of the environment. This interpretation denies individual responsibility for illness. The second stage is the "I/Those" stage, characterized by the initiation of a dialogue with the illness. You accept that there is a relationship between your thoughts and feelings and the changes experienced physically. The third stage is integration, the "I/I" stage, in which you begin to realize "that the disease is you": it is the way you handle your anger, it is the way that you rest or get attention. At this stage you reflect openly on the illness and on yourself and ultimately accept the role you play in becoming ill.

☐ AIDS

The complete destruction of the immune system and the development of any one of several fatal diseases—including a form of cancer, a deadly pneumonia, and other killing fungal bacterial and viral illnesses—is a condition known as Acquired Immune Deficiency Syndrome, or AIDS. It is spreading rapidly both nationally and internationally. In early 1987, the Centers for Disease Control of the Public Health Service estimated that there were about 1.5 million people infected with the AIDS virus, HIV, the human immunodeficiency virus in the United States. Cases are doubling every six to twelve months. Most often the virus attacks seemingly healthy young adults, destroying components of their immune systems, making them susceptible to various opportunistic infections and cancers. The course of the disease is one of progressive deterioration resulting in death, with a mortality rate of approximately 80 percent in two years.

AIDS is more than a physical disease. It is a disease of civilization, of the human condition. It is challenging not only our entire human health system but also our perspectives on sexuality and dying. It is an epidemic unlike any other and will transform our global future in ways we cannot imagine.

It is essential that we not turn away from this grim challenge, that we understand the known and likely causes, and then take steps for control and prevention. There is no longer any doubt that this disease is sexually transmitted or passed through contact with infected blood. It is clearly not casually transmitted. There is no known cure. The control and prevention of this disease is one of the greatest challenges the world faces. The World Health Organization (WHO) has reports on AIDS from 113 countries; it estimates that there are 5 to 10 million people infected. The number is projected to rise to 100 million by 1991. It is the leading cause of death in New York for both men and women in their thirties. AIDS has been compared to the Black Death, which swept Europe from 1347 to 1350, killing some 30 million people out of a population of 75 million in four years.

Conservatively speaking, AIDS may prove to be a key window on the immune system. It appears for AIDS, as with cancer and other illnesses, that if the immune system is in a weakened state, it serves as an invitation to disease. The study of AIDS could help to increase our knowledge of the interaction between disease and the immune system.

In the absence of a cure or vaccine for AIDS, the most enduring and economical intervention is health education promoting behavioral change to ensure prevention of AIDS. This education could possibly incorporate the seven steps on the Healing Path.

While conducting my research for this book, the ever-present question on my mind was, why is it that some people with the same type of terminal diagnosis die, while others go on to apparent cure and good health. This same question begs to be answered with regard to AIDS. The average incubation time for development of AIDS is approximately two years: the estimated median survival time after AIDS develops is twelve months. There is a group of gay men in San Francisco who have been infected with the AIDS virus for five years and have not yet developed the disease. Why?

AIDS antibodies have been exposed to a growing percentage of the population. Far more individuals than those classified as having AIDS have "immunal suppression," a syndrome that can indicate a reduction of our T helper cells and an increase in infection, fatigue, cough, diarrhea, and other symptoms. This has been called AIDS Related Complex (ARC). AIDS and ARC damage our surveillance or immune system. The virus appears to travel on our T helper cells, which normally enhance our immune efficiency.

Dr. Robert Cathcart of Los Altos, California, is attempting to strengthen the immune system by nutritional augmentation. He hypothesizes that the body is depleted by vitamin C when the immune system is under attack, either by substances in the environment, viruses, or any other form of stress. Past research has indicated that persons with high levels of vitamin C intake produce more antibody molecules and also that vitamin C enhances the action of prostaglandin, a hormone-like substance that can help the T lymphocytes and even increase the production of interferon, a substance in the body that can fight the spread of viruses. Dr. Cathcart and other researchers suggest that a bolstering, enhancing, strengthening approach is just as important as the drug approach. If the immune system is the battleground, it is the immune system that needs fortification.

No vaccine has yet been developed to counteract this deadly disease. Perhaps its drug resistance is the result of our previous biological successes. As viruses have built up a resistance to existing drugs, we have not been able to keep up with the shifting targets of fast-changing organisms.

"It is evidently time for a second wave of the Pasteurian revolution. A new level of sophistication is called for in our biomedical skills and in our personal and social behavior if we are able to maintain or recover the freedom from death and disease that was such a glowing hope in the middle of the twentieth century" (Platt, 1987).

☐ BIOFEEDBACK: CHOOSING YOUR OWN REACTIONS

Biofeedback training is another way that you can influence your body's functioning. We have all read accounts of incredible feats of physical control performed by Indian yogis: walking on burning coals without being burned or blistered, being buried in the ground for days and emerging alive, sticking needles into the flesh without bleeding. Such claims are generally assumed to be based on magic or trickery, but a plausible explanation for such feats is that they represent a variation of biofeedback training.

Biofeedback is a technique by which you can make bodily processes, such as heartbeat or skin temperature, perceptible to the senses so that you can manipulate them by conscious mental control. This is accomplished by means of a biofeedback machine that monitors physiological functions and gives visual and/or auditory signals that indicate states of physical functioning. Voluntary control of blood flow, muscle tension, heartbeat, skin temperature, sweat gland activity, and even brain waves—internal physical states that are normally considered to be involuntarily controlled by the autonomic nervous system—have all been shown to be possible using biofeedback. The human nervous system is responsive to voluntary control. This control is effected by a mental construction of the desired physical reality. For example, by imagining that your finger is in a glass of warm water, you can increase the flow of blood to that finger.

Biofeedback techniques demonstrate clearly that every change in your physiological state is accompanied by a corresponding change in your mental/emotional state, conscious or unconscious, and conversely, every change in your mental/emotional state is accompanied by a corresponding change in your physiological state. Each part of our functioning affects the whole self; mind, body, emotions, and spirit are indivisible and interdependent.

Biofeedback has provided the first medically testable evidence that the mind can relieve illness as well as create it. The connection between psychological and physical factors in disease is no longer in question. The necessity of confronting the fears, attitudes, and emotions surrounding illness and of developing strategies by which you might improve your health, however, has not been substantially addressed. As the evidence presented in this chapter shows, attitudes, beliefs, emotions, and personality characteristics are related to health and disease; prolonged chronic stress can influence the immune system; the surveillance theory implies a new concept of personal responsibility for health and disease; and biofeedback research indicates that the mind can relieve illness as well as generate disease. Each of these concepts demonstrates the viability of the interaction between mind and body.

14
HEALING YOURSELF: PART ONE

When I asked Dr. [Albert] Schweitzer how he accounted for the fact that anyone could possibly expect to become well after having been treated by a witch doctor, he said that I was asking him to divulge a secret that doctors have carried around inside them ever since Hippocrates. "But I'll tell you anyway," he said, his face still illuminated by that half-smile. "The witch doctor succeeds for the same reason that all of us succeed. Each patient carries his own doctor inside him. They come to us not knowing that truth. We are at our best when we give the doctor who resides within each patient a chance to go to work." The placebo is the doctor who resides within.—Norman Cousins

Ninety percent of the people who go to the medical profession for help are probably within the range of their body's own healing capabilities.

The word heal means to make whole. We exist within many different and interrelating planes of energy: the material, physical, intellectual, emotional, interpersonal, and spiritual. There may well be others that we have not yet begun to understand. If an imbalance occurs between these levels of energy, sooner or later this imbalance will manifest itself physically. This is called disease. Healing can restore the state of balance between these energy levels.

The ancient physicians called the natural power of the body to control disease the healing power of nature. Somehow this power became veiled in mystery, then was forgotten altogether. Recovery other than that resulting from medicine was called miraculous—or the work of the devil. Healing, however, is not magical nor mysterious; it is natural. What is required is, first, a belief in your body's recuperative and regenerative mechanisms; second, the willingness to let your body be natural; and third, the desire to care for yourself, for your body.

Most of the people who come to me for therapy because they are physically ill have lost touch with their bodies. Consequently they are out of touch with their feelings. It is not surprising that they are diseased. Their symptom or illness is a cry from the body for help.

The suggestions offered in this chapter are given in response to those cries for help and can help you to heal yourself from within.

☐ MONITORING YOUR STRESS REACTION

I described the physiology of stress in Chapter 13. In this chapter, I want to help you assess and, if necessary, change your way of living to help you avoid negative effects from stress.

It has been estimated that more than 80 percent of all disease today is stress-related. There are many ways that you can respond to the stress of modern society: some are productive; others are detrimental to health. It is important to discover the injurious patterns before your health is affected. In order to change your habitual pattern, you must first become *aware* of it.

On a sheet of paper, make four columns. Head each column with one of the following: Personal Stress, Home Stress, Work Stress, and Environmental Stress. Then write down every current stress factor in your life. Problems listed under Personal Stress might include friendship, anxiety, weight gain, low self-esteem, changing values, or spiritual growth. Under Home Stress might be found colicky baby, quarrel with spouse, home repairs, or mortgage payments. Work factors could include career choice, technological change, problems with peers or boss, lack of challenge. Under Environmental Stress elements such as caffeine, food additives, noise, and pollution might appear. Don't forget to include positive stress such as falling in love or winning a lottery! All kinds of stress call for adaptation, even those we experience as joyful.

When you have finished compiling your list, select three or four of the stressful events and let yourself *feel* the reaction you had to them at the time they happened. What did you do about this feeling? How did you feel after that?

We all have to cope with stress and pressure in our daily lives. Some of us appear to thrive on it, while others become ill. A certain amount of stress acts as fuel for achievement and fulfillment; but too much stress not handled well can cause the body's defenses to break down, allowing illness to occur.

"Burnout" is a much-used buzzword today. As a fire consumes itself, so can human beings. The word derives from the experience of dedicated professionals in the helping professions who became frustrated by their clients' demands and bureaucratic red tape, felt they were not appreciated, and ultimately lost their interest, energy, and dedication.

Recent research indicates that where you are on the scale between burnout and peak performance is under your control. What you need for this control is increased self-awareness, a sense of responsibility for self-renewal, and strategies that can be learned and practiced.

The following scale assesses your general level of burnout. It accounts for the personal, social, and work dimensions of your life. Rate yourself from 0 to 5 on each item. On items where things have remained as good as ever or even improved, write yourself 0. On items where things have deteriorated badly, write 5 points. In between rate yourself from 1 to 4.

THE BURNOUT SCALE

1. Do you tire more easily? Feel fatigued rather than energetic? ____
2. Are people annoying you by telling you, "You don't look so well lately"? ____
3. Are you working harder and harder and accomplishing less and less? ____
4. Are you increasingly cynical and disenchanted? ____
5. Are you often invaded by a sadness you can't explain? ____

6. Are you forgetting (appointments, deadlines, personal possessions)? ___
7. Are you increasingly irritable? More short-tempered? More disappointed in the people around you? ___
8. Are you seeing close friends and family members less frequently? ___
9. Are you too busy to do even routine things like make phone calls, read reports, or send out Christmas cards? ___
10. Are you suffering from physical complaints (aches, pains, headaches, a lingering cold)? ___
11. Do you feel disoriented when the activity of the day comes to a halt? ___
12. Is joy elusive? ___
13. Are you unable to laugh at a joke about yourself? ___
14. Does sex seem like more trouble than it's worth? ___
15. Do you have very little to say to people? ___

0–25	You're doing fine
26–35	There are things you should be watching
36–50	You're a candidate
51–65	You're burning out
65+	Take special note, distinct threats to your health and well-being.

Herbert J. Freudenberger and G. Richelson. *Burnout: The High Cost of Achievement.* New York: Bantam Books, 1980.

☐ LISTENING TO YOUR BODY, YOUR FRIEND

We often ignore the messages that come from within our bodies because we have been taught to believe that the responsibility for illness and its cure lies outside of ourselves.

If we were to take the time to listen to the voice that emanates from within, we would find that many of our complaints are manifestations of self-inflicted tension. Imagine your pain or symptom as an important telegram. Your pain is your body insisting that you listen to your needs. If you will let yourself recognize the early signs, you can learn to pace yourself, take time to regroup your energies, and regain the balance in your life. Next time, you can prevent the pain from occurring in the first place.

If you habitually internalize frustration rather than express it and don't share with others your true feelings, you will probably develop recurring ailments from the strain of separating your feelings from your actions. For example, colitis is caused by chronic tension in the lower abdomen. Ulcers, hemorrhoids, and other disturbances of the digestive tract are directly related to tension.

What part of your body is usually affected when you get sick? Is it your throat, stomach, back, or is it several areas? Most of us have a "target area" that usually "gets sick" and breaks down again and again.

Some people get the flu or a cold when they don't want to work but feel guilty for taking time off without an excuse. Is your pet ailment providing this kind of service or function?

Insomnia, chronic constipation, and ongoing muscle stiffness are signals that you are in a state of tension that could be dangerous. The discovery of your particular stress symptoms will help you to make your own diagnosis of your need for relaxation. Then you can make use of some of the exercises in this book to help you heal certain parts of your body.

The following guide lists common physical and emotional symptoms that are partially due to ineffective coping with the pressures and demands of life. Check how frequently you have experienced each of the following symptoms of distress over the past month. Rate yourself on a scale from 3 to 0: 3 for a symptom occurring nearly every day, 2 for one occurring every week, 1 for a symptom occurring once or twice, and 0 for one occurring never. Total your scores.

STRESS SYMPTOMS CHECKLIST*

MUSCULOSKELETAL SYSTEM

1.	Muscle tension	3	2	1	0
2.	Back pain	3	2	1	0
3.	Headaches	3	2	1	0
4.	Grinding teeth	3	2	1	0

GASTROINTESTINAL SYSTEM

5.	Stomach upset	3	2	1	0
6.	Heartburn	3	2	1	0
7.	Vomiting	3	2	1	0
8.	Diarrhea	3	2	1	0
9.	Constipation	3	2	1	0
10.	Abdominal pains	3	2	1	0

OTHER PHYSICAL SYSTEMS

11.	Colds, allergies	3	2	1	0
12.	Chest pains	3	2	1	0
13.	Skin rashes	3	2	1	0
14.	Dry mouth	3	2	1	0
15.	Laryngitis	3	2	1	0
16.	Palpitations	3	2	1	0

TENSION/ANXIETY

17.	Tremors or trembling	3	2	1	0
18.	Twitches or tics	3	2	1	0
19.	Dizziness	3	2	1	0
20.	Nervousness	3	2	1	0
21.	Anxiety	3	2	1	0
22.	Tension and jitteriness	3	2	1	0
23.	Keyed-up feeling	3	2	1	0
24.	Worry	3	2	1	0
26.	Fear of certain objects, phobias	3	2	1	0

ENERGY LEVEL

27.	Fatigue	3	2	1	0
28.	Low energy	3	2	1	0
29.	Apathetic, nothing seems important	3	2	1	0

* Jaffe, D. and C. Scott, *From Burnout to Balance* (New York: McGraw-Hill, 1984) pp. 158-61.

DEPRESSION				
30. Depression	3	2	1	0
31. Fearfulness	3	2	1	0
32. Hopelessness	3	2	1	0
33. Crying easily	3	2	1	0
34. Highly self-critical	3	2	1	0
35. Frustrated	3	2	1	0
SLEEP				
36. Insomnia	3	2	1	0
37. Difficulty awakening	3	2	1	0
38. Nightmares	3	2	1	0
ATTENTION				
39. Accidents or injuries	3	2	1	0
40. Difficulty concentrating	3	2	1	0
41. Mind going blank	3	2	1	0
42. Forgetting important information	3	2	1	0
43. Can't turn off certain thoughts	3	2	1	0
EATING				
44. Loss of appetite	3	2	1	0
45. Overeating, excessive hunger	3	2	1	0
46. No time to eat	3	2	1	0
ACTIVITY				
47. Overwhelmed by work	3	2	1	0
48. No time to relax	3	2	1	0
49. Unable to meet commitments or complete tasks	3	2	1	0
RELATIONSHIPS				
50. Withdrawing from relationships	3	2	1	0
51. Feel victimized, taken advantage of	3	2	1	0
52. Loss of sexual interest or pleasure	3	2	1	0

TOTAL _____

A score over 60 indicates significant stress-related distress, although scores can be inflated by the presence of a chronic medical condition. A score above 40 is cause for some concern and remedial action.

□ RELAXATION

□ Awareness

Are you as aware of your body as you are of your car or television set? Probably not. Yet you regard your body in much the same manner as you would a machine. You fuel it, give it some rest, and even wash and polish it at certain times. Your body is the most wondrous machine. Because it functions so beautifully and with so little care, we make the mistake of taking its functioning for granted. We expect our bodies to operate upon command, and usually they do. Your body will continue to function, even though stressed, with no apparent problem. After extended stress, however, it will start to draw on its reserve energy. If you are listening to your body, it will be sending you some gentle messages, such as an occasional headache, feelings of fatigue, or perhaps some indigestion, to indicate that your resources are low. If you push your body further, it will signal you more urgently, with more severe pain, such as a backache or maybe an ulcer. If you continue to ignore the voices of illness, you can virtually count on a diagnosis such as nervous disorder, cancer, or heart difficulty. The life-giving energy from precious organs such as your lungs, liver, and heart can be sapped.

You can't trade in a used body for a new one. Your body is not just a machine—it is much more. Disease is the consequence of misuse, abuse, and stress. By listening to your body and how it expresses your inner feelings and thoughts, you can learn to recognize your body's malfunctions at a stage when your body can still be healed.

Take a mental snapshot of yourself right now as

you are reading this book. Develop it in your mind's eye. What do you see? Do you appear tired or energetic? Are you breathing lightly or deeply? Are you aware of muscle tension in some parts of your body and not in others?

Your attitude toward your body influences your way of being in this world. Do you hide inside your body? What parts of your body do you like? What do you dislike about your body? Where do your models of physical well-being come from? What parts of your body do you associate with pleasure? What parts of your body are hurtful for you to think about? Are you skimming through these questions, ignoring how you really feel about your body once again? Give yourself a gift. Take the time. Your life, your health, is worth it.

☐ Breathing

Breathing is the most important function for successful relaxation. You are your breath. If you don't breathe, you die. You can breathe life in deeply, or you can hold it away from you by shallow breathing and retaining carbon dioxide, which is a waste product.

Breathing is essential to healing. Breathing is the bridge between your conscious awareness and your unconscious life, between habit and deeper levels of feeling. Deep breathing can unlock repressed feelings and images that may need to be retrieved in order to restore balance.

If you observe your breathing pattern, you can see how your conscious mind interferes with your natural rhythm. As you become aware of your thoughts, your breathing returns to your chest. If you watch a dog, cat, or young child breathing while sleeping, you will observe the most beautiful, natural, undulating muscle ripple from the lower abdomen to the top of the body. The picture is similar to that of a wave moving forward on the ocean. When you are cognitively engaged, in action, or under stress, your breathing comes more from your chest. When you are feeling quiet and restful, it comes more from your abdomen. Both are important, but many of us have lost, through being so busy, the ability to "belly" breathe. Most of us use only a small portion of our lung capacity. By improving our breathing, we can decrease tension and increase energy.

The following relaxation exercise can be done by you alone, or with a friend who can read the steps to you. It would be most helpful if you could record the instructions on a tape recorder and play them back.

The most essential and most difficult part of this exercise is making time to do it. It is a commitment to yourself and to your health. If you do it on a regular basis for at least two weeks, you will notice a remarkable difference in how you feel about yourself.

☐ *Clearing Yourself* Find yourself a room or a place where you can be quiet, alone and uninterrupted. Lie down on the floor in a spot where you can feel safe and secure. Lie on your back with your arms at your sides, palms up, and with your legs uncrossed. The light should be natural or gentle, and, if possible, not fluorescent. If you wish, you can listen to some soft, soothing music.

Gently close your eyes. Gradually become aware of your body. Are you feeling restricted in any way? If you wear glasses, take them off. Loosen your tie, take off your belt and shoes. Feel the difference that this makes. Notice any part of your body that doesn't feel as if it is resting fully on the floor. This might be your lower back, your shoulders, or your legs. Scan your body, becoming aware of any areas that feel particularly uncomfortable. Try to breathe into any tense part, to help it relax. What is that part of your body saying to you?

Now take a few deep breaths. Let the muscles of your abdomen and stomach relax and let your breath sink lower into your body. Place the palm of one hand on your abdomen. Let your hand remain there until you can feel the gentle rise and fall of your breathing. Relax your jaw and open your mouth a little, so that you can exhale through your mouth. Breathe naturally, inhaling through your nose and exhaling through your mouth. Pause at the end of each exhalation, before you breathe again. During the pause, your body will continue to exhale, clearing out the stale air from your lungs and making more room for fresh air. Explore the pause. Is it frightening? Think of your body when you are asleep. Your body knows when to breathe. You can learn to trust your breath.

Now, breathe in fresh air and breathe out carbon dioxide. Breathe in sunshine and breathe out darkness. Breathe in relaxation and breathe out tension. Breathe in bright colors and breathe out blackness. Breathe in joy and breathe out sorrow. Breathe in beauty and breathe out ugliness. Breathe in humor and breathe out bitterness. Breathe in life and breathe out depression. Breathe in hope and breathe out despair. Breathe in health and breathe out disease. Breathe easily and naturally.

Now, let your awareness go to your feet. Become your feet. Move to the soles of your feet. Be aware of the temperature at the bottom of your feet. Feel the texture of your socks or stockings. Be conscious of the spaces in between your toes. Think about how much work your feet do for you. They carry you around all day long. When was the last time you gave them a loving rub? Your feet are your foundation. When you take a "stand," you do it on your feet.

Now move your awareness to your ankles. Be conscious of the intricacies of these structures. Be aware of your ligaments, your Achilles' heel, and the many tiny bones that make up your ankles. Feel the importance of this place, which connects your legs to your feet. Be aware that you make your own connections.

And now move into the calves of your legs. What are you aware of here? Can you feel them relaxing into the floor, or do you have the sensation of them holding up from the floor? Be aware of your shinbone and how thin your skin feels there.

Move to the back of your knees. Let yourself feel how vulnerable you are: how anyone could knock your legs out from under you. We are all this vulnerable from time to time. Move to your kneecaps. Be aware that you do have defenses, and that there are times when you need them to protect yourself.

Move up to your thighs. Who are you in your thighs? Throughout this exercise, please don't judge yourself. Just observe and be aware. Find out who you are without any self-criticism. Can you feel your legs giving in to the floor, letting themselves be supported?

Now let your consciousness go to your buttocks. How much tension are you holding here? Can you relax those muscles? Tell them you want them to let down. Be aware of any feelings that come to you as you energize each area by relaxing. Think about your anus and the essential functions it performs for you. Are there times when you are holding onto things that should be let go?

Now move to your genital area. Who are you here? Do you feel tight, relaxed, firm, soft, dry, wet, open or closed? What are your textures, your colors? How are you feeling as you ask yourself these questions? Are you feeling content, or are you feeling some pangs of sadness or guilt? Let yourself be who you are, and observe.

Now move into your lower abdomen. Concentrate your energy on your intestines. You have the choice to hang on to what you don't need or to let go of it. You can hold in your negative thoughts and feelings or you can go with the flow. Do you have a tendency to constipation? You may have been controlling your body more than you realized.

Let your awareness move to your stomach. Remember that you are what you eat. Are you feeling empty, stuffed, relaxed, or queasy? Have you been nourishing your body or have you been abusing it? Is your stomach churning or are you feeling contentment?

Now move into your chest area. Let yourself become your lungs. Feel yourself expanding and contracting as you breathe in life and breathe out toxins. Feel this natural rhythm, like the waves rolling up on the shore and then retreating into the ocean, taking in and giving out, a universal rhythm to which you move as well. Are you breathing in as much as you want? Are you able to let go of poison? What are you holding back?

Move over to your miraculous heart. You don't just have a heart, you *are* your heart. You are your heartbeat, you are your circulation. Are you sending yourself to all parts of your body; are you reaching your extremities? If there are some parts of your body that feel less alive than others, it may be because there is not enough blood flow to these areas. You can make the difference by sending your awareness and energy to these areas. Try it. **Now.**

Move to your shoulders. Who are you in your shoulders? For most of us, this is a favorite place to store tension. We do it to ourselves, by taking more "on our shoulders" than we can carry with ease. Instead of releasing this tension, we carry it around with us. Imagine the tension in your shoulders as rocks. Imagine the rocks melting, with the help of some kind of radiant heat, taking the form of warm, golden fluid that is gently running down your arms. As the warm fluid passes through your upper arms you can feel those muscles relax. It runs through your elbows into your forearms, and as those muscles let go, the fluid moves through your wrists, into the palms of your hands, and runs right out to your fingertips. Feel the tingling in your hands or the lack of it. The feeling of aliveness will come through practice. Remember, don't judge yourself. Find out about yourself, and then if you decide you want to make some changes, go ahead.

Now move around to your back. Can you feel the two muscles on either side of your backbone resting on the floor? Are you letting the floor support you or are you still trying to hold yourself up? Do you feel you are a person "with backbone" or do you sometimes feel spineless? Do you feel the connection through your spine from your head to your legs?

Move up to your throat and neck. Who are you in your throat? Are you an open channel, facilitating communication between your head and the rest of your body? Are there times when you feel choked or cut off? Do you feel itchy and dry, or do you feel moist and smooth?

Become aware of your jaw. Is it relaxed? Is your mouth slightly open or are you clenching your teeth? Become aware of your lips, your tongue, your teeth, gums, and the lining of your mouth. Become aware of the passageways to your nose and ears. Do these feel blocked in any way? Are you aware of any smells or of the sounds around you? Take a minute to listen to these sounds. Be aware of your internal sounds as well.

Let your attention go to your eyes. Feel your lids resting on your eyes. Be aware of the gray matter that lies behind your eyes, and let that awareness go. Be conscious of the fact that there are times when you have blind spots in your life, and there are other times when you have exceptional vision. Remember that this is all part of being human.

Be aware of all the tiny little muscles surrounding your face and scalp. Imagine them as being stretched tight; now you are going to release them. Now go to the very top of your head. Find out whether you are feeling open here or whether you feel tight and enclosed.

Now be aware of your whole body. You are your body. You are some body, although there may be times when you feel like no-body. Take your hands and run them over your body. This is you. You are your body. Be aware of how you are feeling about yourself as you are touching your body. Notice the places that you are avoiding touching. Take time to explore your body. When you feel finished, put your hands by your side.

Be aware that you are much more than your body. Be conscious of the energy surrounding the outside of your body, your aura. Know that this energy field may expand until it reaches the perimeter of your room and can then extend into your community, the city, the country and the world. Take a few deep breaths and rest quietly for a few moments. Become aware of your breathing and of how your body is feeling—how you are feeling. You can gently open your eyes, get up very slowly, and continue with your day. Or you can go on to the next exercise.

☐ *The Energizer* Find a place where you feel safe, where you will be quiet and uninterrupted. Lie down on your back, on a firm surface with a soft covering. Take several minutes to get in touch with yourself, your body, and how you are feeling. Take a few deep breaths and, during the exhalations, blow away your worries, anxieties, and tension. Continue deep breathing until your body is in a more relaxed state.

Now, send your attention down to your feet. Tighten your feet *for a few seconds* by pointing your toes and curling your feet. Then relax your feet. Tighten them again, but this time extend your heels forward and pull your toes backward and then relax. Do this a few times until you can feel your energy in your feet. Breathe.

Tighten the little muscles around your ankles and hold this for a few seconds, then relax. Breathe.

Tighten your calf muscles, tight, tight, tight, and relax. Breathe.

Stiffen the place behind your knees and hold it tight and then relax. Breathe.

Tighten your thighs. Hold them very tight and then relax. Breathe. What sensations are you aware of now in your legs? Do they feel lighter? Are they tingling or do they feel wooden? Are you more aware of one leg than the other? Give your legs a little shake and then breathe.

Now tighten your buttocks and your anus. Come on, you can lift them off the floor more than that! Hold them tight, tight, tight, and relax. Breathe.

Now squeeze your genitals. Hold for a few seconds. Relax and breathe. Wiggle your hips around a little. What are you aware of feeling as you do this? Breathe.

Bend your knees a little and place your feet flat on the floor. Now raise your hips off the ground as high as you can. Lower them back to the floor. Do this five or six times. Be aware of any sensations, feelings, or thoughts. Breathe.

Tighten the muscles in your lower abdomen. You can do this by flexing them or by pulling them in toward your back. Hold hard for a few seconds and then relax. Breathe.

Now tighten all the muscles in your stomach. Hold,

hold, hold, and then relax. Breathe.

Now compress all the muscles in your chest. Hold this, tight, tight, tight, and let go. And breathe. Fill your lungs to full capacity and then exhale completely. Do this several times.

Direct your attention to your back. Contract the muscles in your back. Hold this, tight, tight, tight, and relax. Try this again. Sometimes it is difficult to locate, isolate and tense certain muscles. Breathe.

Now move up to your shoulders. Raise your shoulders up to your ears. Come on, you can raise them even higher. Hold for a few seconds and relax. Feel what you are feeling now in your shoulders. Because this is a favorite storage place for tension, you will probably be aware of the change in your shoulders. Repeat this several times, enjoying your increased relaxation. Breathe and smile. Now, pull your shoulders down as far as you can, extending the back of your neck upward. Relax and breathe. Wiggle your shoulders around. Breathe.

Raise your right arm. Make your right hand into a fist. Flex your right bicep just as hard as you can. If you feel like making a sound, do so. Now stretch your forearm by undoing your fist and pulling your fingers back over your wrist. Now make the fingers of your hand into a claw. Be aware of any aggressive feelings like clawing or scratching. Breathe. Repeat this exercise with your left arm and hand. Breathe. Shake out your hands, wrists, and arms.

Be aware of your jaw. Clench your teeth and let yourself emit a little growl, or even a big growl. Don't be afraid to make your sound, it's just you, giving yourself permission to let go of some tension. Growl a few times, experimenting with your sound and how this makes you feel. Now open your mouth as wide as you can, even wider. How do you feel as you are doing this? At the same time open your eyes wide. Are you aware of any fear or amazement? Breathe.

Without using your hands, give yourself a facial massage. Wiggle your nose, eyes, mouth, and even your ears into as many different shapes and formations as possible. Keep moving them, giving your face a real workout. Now stop and feel the difference in your face. Feel your tingling and aliveness. Breathe.

Give your eyes some special treatment. Squeeze them shut and then relax them without opening. Do this several times, being aware of any changing sensation or colors. Breathe.

Now try to get hold of all the tiny muscles around your face and scalp. Flex them and relax them several times. Breathe. Move your head gently as if you were saying a silent "no," several times. Then move your head gently as if you were saying "yes." Breathe.

Let yourself be indulgent and really enjoy the next step of this exercise. I'm going to count slowly to three. On the count of three, I want you to tense every muscle in your body, pull your knees to your chest, pull your head to your knees, clench your fists and teeth, and hold your breath. Allow yourself to have a mini temper tantrum. As I count to three, breathe in; on the count of three, hold your breath and tighten every muscle.

One, two, THREE! Tighten every muscle! Hold your breath! Hold on, don't give in, don't give in, don't give in, and then, RELAX! UNFOLD! and BREATHE! Do this again if you wish. You will learn to enjoy it!

Be aware of how you are feeling in your body. What feels different? Are you aware of feeling alive in some parts and dead in other parts? How are you feeling emotionally?

This exercise can be a great energizer. You can start the day off with it, or you can use it as a refresher during the day. You can adjust it to suit your particular situation. You can do it sitting at your desk or waiting for the subway. You will derive most benefit, however, by making a special time and going to a special place: doing so helps to make you feel special.

☐ CENTERING WITH THE GOLDEN LIGHT

There is an energy available to us in our universe about which we know very little. It has been described in various ways. The Japanese call this power "Ki" or universal spirit. They perceive this as an actual molecular substance, an energy that moves and can be channeled, focused, or "centered" in different parts of the body. It is the same concept as the *Chi* ("Absolute") in Tai Chi Chuan. When you are centered, you feel at ease, in harmony, clear, and strong. Centering is directly related to good health and self-healing.

Sit in a comfortable chair or find a soft but firm place to lie down. Take a few minutes to calm yourself, close your eyes, and get in touch with your breathing. Scan your body. Become aware of any areas that are particularly tense. Breathe strongly into these places, commanding them to relax. Then let your breathing return to your normal, regular rhythm.

Gradually let yourself become aware of a source of energy emanating from deep within your body. Imagine this to be in the general area of your solar plexus. As you become aware of your center, imagine that the energy radiating from it is giving off a beautiful, soft, golden glow. As you breathe in, the golden color deepens in intensity; as you breathe out, the light dims. As you continue to breathe this golden light continues to expand. Each breath you take makes the light a little brighter and warmer.

Imagine this light and warmth radiating out from your center in all directions. As it moves it caresses you, soothing all parts of your body with its gentle warmth and energy. Each part of your body glows and is warmed as you send this golden light throughout your body. Feel your body becoming peaceful and relaxed. Breathe gently and peacefully.

Open your eyes slowly. Take a few minutes to get back in touch with your physical environment. Don't rush off after doing this exercise. Take some time to be in touch with yourself and how you are feeling.

Be conscious of the fact that you achieved a state of relaxation and have given yourself a gift. You can do this for yourself many times in many different settings. This exercise is a form of self-hypnosis, and you can achieve very beneficial results by using it.

☐ MEDITATION

Meditation has been called the royal road to healing. Its purpose is to bring you into a state of calm, warmth, balance and renewed energy. It helps you to contact your deeper self, your soul or wisdom. This contact helps to guide you in your healing process.

Meditation has beneficial physiological effects. It helps to decrease stress and reduce muscle tension. It regulates and slows respiration. It helps to decrease blood pressure and slow the heart. It lowers one's rate of metabolism. It brings about peace of mind and body.

Sit in a comfortable position where you are not likely to go to sleep. The best time for a relaxation exercise is before eating. Many people prefer the early morning, just after rising and before breakfast. Your environment should be quiet, without interruption. Have someone else look after small children.

Take the phone off the hook. Make sure that you are in a position that you can hold without moving for a few minutes. Slowly close your eyes. Check your body for any discomfort. If you find a tense area, breathe into it and on exhalation release the tension and relax the muscles.

Pay attention to the world outside yourself. Listen to the sounds. Do you allow yourself to become part of that "rat race" out there too often? For the next few moments let go of it. Become aware of your present environment. Feel the temperature of the room right next to your skin. What else are you aware of in this room? Order? Chaos? Restfulness? Now move inside your skin. What physical sensations are you aware of? What sounds are you aware of inside your body?

Pay attention to your breathing. Get in touch with the basic rhythm of your breathing. Follow your breath. Go with your breath as it enters your nose, goes down your throat and deep into your lungs. Feel your belly and chest expand and your shoulders rise. Follow your breath on exhalation. As the carbon dioxide flows from your lungs, through your throat, and out your open mouth, be aware of your chest relaxing and your shoulders letting down. Continue to concentrate on your breathing.

Your mind will wander from time to time, and unbidden thoughts will pull at your concentration. Let these thoughts enter your mind, recognize them, gently send them on their way, and bring your concentration back to your breathing. This will happen many times. The important thing is to remain calm and uncritical and simply let your thoughts pass through. You know you can attend to them later.

You might find counting helpful. As you inhale, count one, and as you exhale, count two. Continue to do this up to ten, and then start at one again. Continue to meditate. Stay with it only as long as you are comfortable, perhaps five minutes. Gradually you can extend your time to ten or twenty minutes, once or twice a day.

You might like to change from the counting technique to selecting a particular object for concentration. This could be a mandala (a circle enclosing a symbolic pattern), a flower, a tree, or some other object that you find attractive. To do this, select a quiet spot, sit with your spine erect (get a back support if you need one), and give your selected object your undivided attention. Your eyes will be open of course. Let yourself identify with your object. For example, if you have selected a tree, let yourself become the tree. How sturdy are you, how tall? Are you firmly rooted? What kind of soil are you growing in? What are your surroundings? Do you get enough air, sunlight, and water? Have you enough space? What kind of foliage do you have? What season is it? How do these qualities of the tree relate to you? Stay with your attention on the tree for about ten minutes.

Gently say good-bye to the tree. Bring your attention back to your body, getting in touch with your breathing. Know that you are physically and mentally alert. Be aware of the rhythm of your breathing. Know that you are in charge of yourself—your body. Be with yourself for a few minutes: take time to feel.

Give yourself a wonderful, complete body stretch. Shake out any tight areas of your body. You should feel refreshed and revitalized.

The main purpose of meditation is to achieve a state of combined relaxation and alertness. Because it is a learned technique, it is essential that you practice meditation regularly. It is a way of training your body to regenerate. It helps if you select a regular time and place and make it your own healing oasis.

☐ IMAGERY

Imagery is probably our most ancient and potent resource for healing. It is an enterprise that calls forth all our senses: vision, sound, taste, smell, touch, and the sense of movement or position. It is a tool that helps us to tap into our unconscious and our superconscious (from which we receive artistic, philosophical, humane, and heroic inspiration). Imagery is the wordless language of the body.

You can use imagery to alter negative expectancies of the outcome of your disease, and images can be used to reinforce your positive expectations. Mental images can help you effect profound physiological change. When you recall and imagine special scenes from the past, you can sometimes evoke the very same smells, sights, and sounds that were connected to the event. You can also cause change in your blood pressure, brain waves, and muscles. Your imagination is extremely fertile and powerful.

I am discussing "imagery" rather than "visualization" because not everyone is able to visualize. Approximately 60 percent of people image in ways different from visualization. They hear, smell, or feel images—or even become aware of them without what are known as sensory clues.

The process of imagery cloaks itself in pictures that are unique for each individual. They arise from within, appear for a purpose, and are deeply meaningful.

My client Sarah was suffering from pain in her chest area and was having difficulty with some personal relationships. I asked her to take some deep breaths and helped her relax her body. Then I asked her to go inside her body to her heart, and to get some feeling for her heart by observing it with all her senses. I then instructed her to leave her heart and to let a symbol emerge on her inner screen that would represent her heart. Her symbol appeared quickly and clearly.

It was a beautiful, large, shining harp made of gold. She said, "It looks like a heart, or at least half a heart. Perhaps the music makes up the other half."

Sarah thought about her harp and what it meant to her:

> A harp plays wonderful music. Its capacity for beauty is endless, yet it also has the capacity to be abused. Sometimes I let my strings get plucked abusively, by myself and other people. I can play them in time to the pulse of life, and I can allow others to play them this way, too. I am aware when others play them and that they only do it with my permission, not because they are in control.
>
> The strings of my harp lie uniformly beside each other. When one is plucked, it quivers separately. The others sense and feel it, but they do not move, as they are strings unto themselves. These strings are my different parts. When one responds, the others can remain still and help balance the moving parts. When more or all the strings are plucked, I can be in agony or ecstasy. I am temporarily out of "sync." In that ecstasy or agony, when all my strings are being plucked, comes a beautiful music—the joy of life!

After the imagery, Sarah noticed that her pain was gone and she felt peaceful inside.

Imagery allows you the opportunity to get in touch with your soul, providing the window for your soul to have access to you. Illness has been described as the result of not being transparent to the soul. Imagery may be your journey to health made visible.

☐ Imagery as a Healing Technique

You may do this exercise either lying down or sitting up. It is important to position yourself so that you will not fall asleep—and if you do fall asleep, ask yourself if you are avoiding your body and why. It would be helpful if you could dictate these instructions to a tape recorder and then play them back for yourself any time. The exercise will take about half an hour.

First, do the deep breathing and relaxation exercise described earlier in this chapter. As a variation, you might like to imagine that the top of your head is open to all the life forces in the universe and that the bottoms of your feet have plugs in them that you have taken out. Breathe in the fresh and energizing air. As it flows through your head, let it soothe away the tension in the muscles around your eyes, mouth, and cheeks. Let them relax. As you exhale, imagine that tension flowing down through your body and out the bottoms of your feet. Keep breathing in this universal life force, letting it bathe each area of your body progressively down to your feet. Include your neck muscles, shoulders, back, arms and hands, chest, stomach, abdomen, internal organs, buttocks, genitals, thighs, knees, calves, ankles, feet, and toes. Do this very slowly, taking time to soothe and care for every part of your body. Keep the flow going from top to bottom, from head to toe.

Take a few deep breaths and let a sound come with your exhalation. Feel your release of tension.

Now, find in your mind's eye a place in nature that is full of healing energy. It might be a deserted beach in the Caribbean, a grassy field in the country, a still northern lake or forest, or a hammock in your own back yard. Choose a place that feels safe for you and where you won't be interrupted.

When you have arrived in this place, slow down. Use all your senses. How does it look, what do you smell, what can you touch and feel? Walk around in this place and make it your own. Select an especially comfortable spot and get ready to proceed with this exercise.

Think of a place in your body that has been trying to get your attention lately by signaling a disturbance. The signal could be a headache, a backache, a rash, or feelings of indigestion. Anyone, anytime, can find some area of his or her body that could be improved. You might become aware of a recurring infection, a feeling of numbness, or a diagnosed disease.

Make your psychic self very, very tiny. Shrink yourself, just as Alice in Wonderland did, until you are microscopic. Now select one of the orifices of your body and enter your body through it. Move right in until you become aware that you are riding along on your bloodstream. Don't be afraid. This is your body and this trip is being taken on your behalf, for your own good health. Let yourself flow along with your circulation, until you arrive at the place in your body that has been causing you pain or irritation.

Get off your bloodstream and look about. What do you see or sense? Imagine that you are the foreperson on the job here, and that it is up to you to assess this place in your body and decide what needs to be done. Don't be inhibited by anatomical detail. Use your creative imagination and give yourself permission to exaggerate. How much damage is there? Is there an abnormality in size, color, or texture? Are you aware of any smell? Is there damage in the bone, the tissue, or in anything else? How much repair is needed, and how long will it take?

Now is the time to call upon your natural recuperative mechanisms. Summon your immune system, your white blood cells. Breathe in oxygen and stimulate your circulation. Tell these healing helpers what needs to be done and give them some direction as to how they should proceed. When they are well under way, turn to the realm of invention.

Now call upon imaginary beings to come to help you repair this area of your body. These may be human, animal, mechanical, fantasy, or whatever your imagination dreams up. Give yourself permission to summon to your aid some kind of wonderful help (knights on white horses, vacuum cleaners, laser beams). Take charge. Instruct your help to unwind the squeezed muscle, to remove diseased cells, or to chip away at bony overgrowth. Get them working at whatever needs to be done. Think of a way to rid yourself of old or diseased cells and tissue. Flush them out of your system. If your workers seem sluggish, give them a pep talk. Liven them up. Make them well aware just how much you want your body to be in good working condition.

After a while, make another assessment of your body. Do you see any change? Has the color improved, swelling or inflammation abated? Has your pain decreased or even disappeared? Tell your workers that they may stop for now, but that you will be calling upon them again before long. Thank them for their contribution to your improved health. Tell this area on which you have been working that you will keep returning until it has been healed.

Before you leave, give this part of your body a voice. Ask it for an explanation as to why it is not functioning properly. Listen carefully to what it tells you. Ask for any further information. Inform your body that you are going to listen to what it has to tell you and give it better care.

Now prepare to leave. Make sure everything is cleaned up or discarded. Find a way to say good-bye to this part of your body. Jump back onto your circulatory system and travel back through your body until you reach the orifice through which you entered. Make your exit and grow yourself back to normal size. How do you feel? You probably notice some changes. Imagine yourself with no symptoms, no pain, no illness. Imagine how you would feel. Imagine what you could do with your life!

Give yourself lots of time to come out of this exercise. It is quite a trip! Put your hands over the place in your body that you were visiting and hold them there for a few minutes. Caress the rest of your body with your hands. Listen to and feel your breathing. Do all this before opening your eyes. Then gently open your eyes and rest quietly before moving. When you get up, move slowly for the first little while. For the rest of the day try to maintain some of the relaxed feeling you have achieved.

☐ Finding Your Inner Guide

Meeting your guide will connect you with your intuition and your wisdom. Your inner guide is sometimes called your spirit guide or imaginary friend. It is also known as a higher part of yourself or a connection with universal intelligence. Your guide usually comes in the form of a being who relates to you in a wise and loving way.

Read the instructions into a tape recorder and play it back for yourself, or have a friend read them to you. Otherwise, read this through yourself, then close your eyes and do the exercise.

Make yourself comfortable in a place where you will be quiet and uninterrupted. Take a few minutes to detach yourself from the outside world and to say hello to your inside world. Breathe deeply as in the other exercises. Imagine a warm ball of light entering your left foot and slowly traveling up your leg. As it passes through each muscle, your muscle gradually releases tension. If the warm ball of light gets stuck, that particular muscle has not relaxed. Breathe into your muscle until it does relax. Let the golden ball travel through your other leg and then through your whole body until you are feeling totally relaxed. Then let it disappear.

Imagine yourself in a beautiful, natural environment. It can be any place that appeals to you: on a mountaintop, by the sea, even on another planet. Explore this place, becoming aware of sounds, smells, visual detail and any special feelings that arise in you. Change this environment in any way you wish to make it more comfortable and more your own. This is your private sanctuary. It is a safe place where you can relax and heal.

If you look carefully, you will see a path leading out from your sanctuary and winding away off into the distance. It winds so far away that you can't see where it ends. As you look down this path, you become aware of shimmering light particles in the distance. They are a bluish-white color. This mass of light appears to be coming closer. As it moves along the path toward you it begins to take shape. You are becoming excited and feel no fear. As it comes closer, you are able to distinguish a form. It may be a human being, an animal, a bird, or a fantasy figure. Now you can make out the face: guess how old this creature is and see what it is wearing. The closer it gets, the more details you can see.

Greet this being and find out its name. You feel safe and friendly toward this energy form, as if you have known it for a long time. Introduce it to your sanctuary, explore it together. Your guide may point out some details of which you were unaware. You are enjoying each other's company.

Sit down together. Taking your guide's hand in yours, ask it something you have been wanting to know for some time. Wait for the answer and listen carefully. Ask for any additional information you want. Ask if there is any particular wisdom or advice your guide has for you.

When the experience of being together feels complete for now, thank this wise friend and ask it to visit you again. Say good-bye and watch your guide return up the path, gradually dissolving into bluish-white shimmering light and finally disappearing.

Know that you can re-create this experience any time you wish, that you can visit with your guide at your command. Your guide is there for you when you need extra direction, inspiration, wisdom, love, or companionship. Some people meet their guides every day in their meditation. You can, too. Your guide may change form and name from time to time. It may have a sense of humor or an eccentric or dramatic flair. Your creative imagination is powerful and limitless. Enjoy it!

15
HEALING YOURSELF: PART TWO

To keep life we must strengthen all our links with life and living. Active participation in life has no substitute.
—Arnold A. Hutschnecker

This chapter describes ways to help you heal yourself by strengthening your own propensities for healing through actions involving something or someone other than yourself. These include exercise, nutrition, psychotherapy, massage, creative and aesthetic growth, and spiritual development.

☐ EXERCISE

We all well know of the physical benefits that come from daily exercise. Swimming, working out, and running or jogging are probably the most popular forms of exercise; however, you need to pick an activity that suits you physically and really gives you pleasure.

However, before embarking on any program of physical exercise, it is wise to consult with your doctor to determine the activity's suitability for you in terms of your overall fitness and general state of health. Swimming is my favorite exercise. The feel of the water is refreshing and cleansing. As I swim my lengths, I keep count, and this practice has evolved into a kind of meditation with regular breathing. I have also found that it encourages my creative thinking. Many of the ideas for this book took shape as I swam and counted, length after length.

For many, jogging is the most convenient and enjoyable form of exercise; like swimming, it promotes not only physical health but also emotional and mental well-being. Jogging can help you to lose weight, tone your muscles, and, because it increases blood circulation, tighten your skin. Emotions become less subject to irritation, and your mental and physical capacity for work will probably increase. By focusing on the physical realities of jogging, you steady your mind. Jogging can be a wonderful way to let go of daily turmoil and revitalize yourself with fresh air and interesting scenery.

There are some conditions that may warrant special medical guidance with respect to jogging: heart disease and hypertension, advanced arthritis, some orthopedic problems, and diabetes.

Whenever you jog, start slowly, giving your body

time to warm up. This will allow your blood vessels to expand and your blood to circulate more freely. Concentrate on your breathing, making it deep and regular. Develop a rhythm that suits your stride. Focus your attention on body awareness and inner experience rather than on how fast or how far you can jog. Jogging can become a form of meditation.

When you come to the end of your jog, take time to wind down by doing some stretching exercises. Jog regularly. With regular practice your body will become less heavy, firmer, and better able to handle stress.

Physical inactivity is probably the greatest stressor on your body. You can relieve this stress by incorporating an enjoyable and healthy exercise program into your daily life. I can already hear the cries of resistance: "I don't have the time, I don't like being in a class, I can't afford expensive equipment, it takes too long to get there, instruction is too costly, and besides I feel too self-conscious."

Do I have the exercise for you? An emphatic yes! It doesn't cost you anything. You do it on your own time, at your convenience, and you don't need any equipment. It is the world's oldest form of aerobic exercise and it is probably the best. Have you guessed? It is **walking**.

Walking helps to prevent heart disease; it can relieve the pain of angina and ease the pain of arthritis; as well, it can help reverse some of the physical aspects of aging.

Walking has more effect on weight loss than dieting. A group of obese people who had failed to lose weight by dieting were asked to continue their normal eating habits and to walk at least thirty minutes a day for a year. At the end of the year each of these people had lost an average of twenty-two pounds.

Walking helps rid the body of fat, whereas dieting

can cause the loss of lean body tissue. With walking, you won't suffer the decrease in metabolic rate that accompanies severe caloric restriction. Stringent dieting can result in fewer calories being burned up, while walking helps to increase the metabolic rate. The ideal combination is to combine sensible eating habits with an aerobic exercise such as walking, jogging, or swimming.

Several of my clients came for therapy following heart attacks. I recommended that they include walking in their strategies for healing. They discovered that, not only were they walking off their unwanted pounds, they were also being good to their hearts. Many cardiologists are now incorporating walking into special cardiac-rehabilitation programs. They feel that walking is the ideal method for a convalescing individual to rebuild strength. The American Heart Association suggests that you may be able to prevent a future heart attack by walking.

Walking can help to halt or prevent osteoporosis, the loss of minerals that causes bones to become porous and brittle. It has also been known to slow down degenerative changes in the joints and to prevent or relieve symptoms of rheumatoid arthritis. It can strengthen your immune system by increasing your white blood cell count.

A group of Canadian men and women in their midsixties were given endurance training that emphasized vigorous walking. The results of this training were a decrease in body fat, increased flexibility in the knees, increased body levels of potassium (a metallic element required for most physiological functions), and an apparent halt to the normal age-related loss of bone calcium.

You will often feel that you have more energy after walking. It seems that walking promotes increased endorphin production (endorphins are neurohormones that promote a sense of well-being). My clients have found that walking helps to relieve, or at least reduce, depression. The rhythm of walking and the movement through space somehow helps you to see your problems in a different light. Walking can help you to feel more hopeful.

All you need to set up your own daily walking program is a pair of comfortable, flexible walking (or running) shoes, preferably ones with cushioned soles. Start off gently, building up to your own comfortable pace. You can reconnect yourself with nature as you walk by finding a park, a ravine, or a country road that you can visit often, observing the seasonal changes in flowers, shrubs, and trees. You can provide yourself with a feeling of freedom and expansion and an opportunity to be alone. The feeling of sunshine or rain on your skin, the experience of fresh air in your lungs, the sounds of wildlife, and the smell of the earth are all rejuvenating.

We now know that exercise does stimulate the immune system and channel the psychological effects of stress. It helps to create psychological change. People on regular exercise programs "tend to be more flexible in their thinking and beliefs, they tend to have an increased sense of self-sufficiency, a strengthened self-concept, improved self-acceptance, less tendency to blame others, and less depression. The overall picture is that people engaged in regular exercise programs tend to develop a healthier psychological profile in general—one often identified with a favorable prognosis for the course of malignancy" (Simonton, Matthews-Simonton, and Creighton, 1980).

☐ NUTRITION

We know now that every cell in the body is replaced over a period of seven years. The new cells are made up of the nourishment taken into the body. You are, literally, what you eat.

There is an abundance of information on diet and nutrition on the market. The viewpoints presented are so diverse, however, that you may become more confused than you were before you began to read about nutrition. Your own inner body wisdom is your best guide in developing a diet that will optimize your physical, mental, and spiritual well-being. It is important to keep in mind that there is not one right way to eat. *Your* metabolism and *your* energy needs are different from those of others.

Sensitivity to the needs of your body takes time and effort to develop. Sometimes your body signals are caused by habit rather than by genuine bodily need. For example, you may crave something sweet when actually your body would benefit more from some protein or even a walk. This stage of learning is transitional; as you continue to experiment, you will gradually develop an informed sensitivity to the foods you need to nourish your body-mind-spirit.

Nutrition is one of your best weapons against cancer. You can reduce your cancer risk by *one-third*, right now, by making simple dietary changes. No cancer screening program or medical or surgical intervention can cite prevention figures anywhere close to this. In a 1982 report to the National Cancer Institute, the National Academy of Sciences stated: "About 35 percent of all cancers can be prevented simply by changing the foods we eat. Most common cancers are preventable. By controlling what we eat we may prevent diet-sensitive cancers, an easier task than curing them after they have taken hold."

Recent research indicates that the proportion of cancers related to diet is even larger than that related to smoking (even though smoking contributes to 30 percent of all cancers in the United States today). Scientists estimate that diet plays a key role in more than 133,000 American cancer deaths a year: 51,000 from colorectal cancer, 37,000 from breast cancer, 25,000 from prostate cancer, and 20,000 from cancers of the mouth, throat, larynx, and esophagus.

There are natural chemical carcinogens in many food plants, but they are counterbalanced by a wide range of nutrients that help prevent cancer. The key is to eat more cancer-preventive foods and at the same time avoid substances known to promote the disease. It is an unhappy truth that carcinogens are now so prevalent in the environment that they are disturbing this ancient balance. Fortunately, however, we can fortify our defenses against cancer with improved nutrition.

Most cancers take many years before they produce detectable symptoms. You read earlier in this book that your body produces cancer cells every day and that, if your immune system is functioning properly, it will destroy these cancer cells and inhibit further cancer-causing biochemical changes.

The armories of our defense system require specific nutrients to function effectively. These include beta-carotene (the plant precursor of vitamin A), vitamin C, vitamin E, and the mineral selenium. Fiber and a class of substances called "indoles" found in vegetables of the cabbage family are also powerful cancer preventives.

The following is adapted from M. Roffers, "How to Fight Cancer with Your Fork."

☐ *Vitamin A* Beta-carotene is found in dark yellow, orange, and green fruits, in particular, apricots and cantaloupe, and in vegetables such as carrots, leaf lettuce, asparagus, and broccoli. It helps to prevent cancers of the epithelial tissue, which forms your skin and the linings of your lungs, esophagus, stomach, intestines, and colon. (Lung and colorectal cancers cause the highest incidence of death.)

☐ *Vitamin C* This potent vitamin is found primarily in citrus fruits, green peppers, cantaloupe, and broccoli. It is associated with a low incidence of cancers of the esophagus, stomach, bladder, and colon.

Vitamin C also helps to control the effects of food high in nitrates. These include foods that have been pickled, cured, or smoked—foods such as bacon, luncheon meats, and smoked fish, ham, and turkey. Sodium nitrite is used widely as a food preservative. Epidemiological evidence indicates that foods high in nitrites contribute to esophagus and stomach cancer, and that, even when nitrite-containing foods are eaten, vitamin C helps to prevent these illnesses.

Ensuring a sufficient intake of vitamin C is especially important for smokers because they use up vitamin C much faster than nonsmokers. Vitamin C has been shown to reduce the risk of cancers of the mouth and esophagus.

☐ *Vitamin E and Selenium* Vitamin E prevents fats and oils from becoming rancid. High-fat diets are strongly linked to cancers of the colon and breast. Vitamin E protects cell membranes.

Selenium plays a similar biochemical role and also protects cell membranes. Public health officials in China added selenium and vitamin E to the diets of a group of people whose throat cells showed precancerous cell changes. The result was 40 percent less throat cancer than was expected. Selenium and vitamin E seem to enhance each other's cancer-preventative properties. (Selenium can be toxic at high levels, and should be used only under the supervision of a doctor.)

Most cancer-preventative nutrients work together and must be present together to be effective. Happily for all of us, they are contained together in whole grains and fresh fruits and vegetables.

☐ *Fiber & Indoles* Fiber is particularly effective in the prevention of colorectal cancer. In cultures with high-fiber diets, colon cancer is rare. In Western society, with its low-fiber white bread, white rice, and white-flour-based baked goods, colorectal cancer is quite common.

Many cancer-prevention authorities recommend *doubling* the amount of fiber in the average North American diet. You can do this by eating one or two servings a day of coarse fibers such as wheat bran, bran cereals, shredded wheat or oats, or bulgur wheat.

Indoles are cancer inhibitors found in high concentrations in vegetables of the cabbage family, the cruciferous vegetables—broccoli, brussels sprouts, cabbage, and cauliflower. Indoles help to protect the body against stomach and colorectal cancer.

☐ *Fat* One of the major sources of carcinogens in the diet is fat. Few people appreciate the fact that dietary fat is a major risk factor for colorectal and breast cancer, which kill a total of almost ninety thousand people a year in the United States alone.

Substantial research indicates that *all* fats, not just saturated fats, increase significantly the risk of breast and colon cancer.

Since dietary fat is strongly associated with cancer, it is not surprising that obesity is, too. A twelve-year study conducted by the American Cancer Society showed that women weighing 40 percent more than their recommended weight developed cancer 55 percent more frequently than women of normal weight. Men similarly overweight showed an excess cancer rate 33 percent higher than normal.

☐ *Food Additives* Whenever possible, you should avoid food additives suspected of being carcinogenic. These include the nitrites, saccharin, and artificial colors. Red dye Number 40, commonly used in sodas, candy, baked goods, and gelatin desserts, is the most harmful.

Fortunately, many cancer-fighting nutrients come packaged in the same foods. Asparagus, broccoli, brussels sprouts, and beans, for example, all have moderate-to-high levels of fiber, indoles, and vitamins A and C.

Another way to improve your diet is to avoid cooking with polyunsaturated oils. Avoid deep-fried dishes and fatty cuts of meat. Chicken and potatoes can be baked, and any food that is usually sautéed can be cooked by simmering in broth, wine, vegetable and fruit juices, or a mixture of water and herbs. Barbecuing and charbroiling deposit carcinogens on food; try some other methods of cooking. Vegetables should be eaten fresh. When cooked, they should be steamed rather than boiled in order to preserve nutrients.

These cooking suggestions, combined with reducing total fat intake, avoiding food additives, limiting consumption of alcohol, and not smoking, can significantly tip the cancer-promotion/cancer-prevention balance in the direction of prevention.

The Canadian Cancer Society has stated that high-fiber, low-fat diets can decrease the risk of cancer. They advise an increase in fresh fruit and vegetables and a reduction of salt, fat, and smoked and cured meats.

The old adages "eat a well-balanced diet" and "everything in moderation" still hold true. Good nutrition, one of the keys to the prevention of cancer and of illness in general, lies in *your* hands.

☐ PSYCHOTHERAPY

The search for health eventually becomes a search for self. The results of my own experiences with illness, and the changes I have witnessed in my clients and in the people interviewed for this book have convinced me that each person possesses the constructive potential for self-realization. By self-realization, I mean the discovery and fulfillment of your unique capabilities. This concept is supported by other authors such as Abraham Maslow and Rollo May. Psychoanalyst Eric Fromm put the same idea into an ethical framework by saying that the duty to be alive is the same as the duty to become yourself.

This potential for growth often becomes stunted, constricted, or blocked, and our inability to express our essential selves openly and freely is translated into personality problems and/or physical disease. Maslow has suggested that these problems may be loud protests against the crushing of our psychological bones, of our true nature. Your body speaks: the voice is illness. The need for growth is expressed through a physical metaphor.

Individuals suffering from constricted growth can often be rescued and rejuvenated through the process of psychotherapy. The first step is to realize that you do need help, and the second step is to find the kind of help that you need. Finding someone you can trust, someone who can be there for you in a way that perhaps no one ever has been before, can be lifesaving and even life giving.

The focus of your therapy will be on personal growth rather than on physical cure or recovery; the purpose is to discover the blocked areas of energy in your body, so that this energy may be released to help your body heal. These blocks have usually taken place at an unconscious level through fear, loss, or misunderstanding. At the time a block was created, it may have been a defense necessary for survival, but that time has passed and the illness in your body is telling you that something in your psychological makeup needs to change.

Psychotherapy can help you to further understand and express yourself and your potential, it can increase your knowledge of the matrix of your disease—the stress, loss, or conflict that played a part in its growth—and it can help you to develop strategies and a suitable lifestyle to maintain your health and prevent illness.

Psychotherapy based on the stages of Personal Agency or the Healing Path assists in the journey to health in the following manner:

☐ *Awareness* The first step helps you to increase your awareness of what your beliefs and attitudes really are toward cancer or any other kind of illness. You share and discuss with your therapist your thoughts and feelings about living and dying.

Cancer is often perceived as the "Big Killer." If you have been given a diagnosis of cancer, you may very well find yourself surrounded by people (including your doctor), whose attitudes demonstrate hopelessness and depression. For your own peace of mind, it is essential that you get honest information about the nature of your illness. Only then can you maintain the firmness of your own convictions and not be unduly influenced by gloomy and less informed people. It is imperative that you obtain accurate and up-to-date medical information in order to help you to make *informed* decisions about the direction of your health.

Part of your increased awareness includes the understanding that, contrary to commonly held belief, disease does not just happen from the outside; it often results from unresolved inner conflict. You also learn that cancer cells are destructible and are, in fact, weak, confused cells. Increase your appreciation of your own efficient immune system and learn how you can help to keep it strong and efficient.

☐ *Meaning* Most of us do not really understand the meaning of living or dying until we are faced with illness or the death of someone close. It is difficult to appreciate that there is no meaning to life except that which we give it. It is hard to give up wanting someone or something outside ourselves to give meaning, and it takes strong and determined effort to develop a meaningful life.

The individuals interviewed for this book told me that it was the news that their illnesses were terminal that forced them to re-evaluate their lives. My clients had to look closely at themselves and their lives to find the meanings of their illnesses. Questions they asked themselves were: "In what ways did I contribute to getting sick? Why did I contract this particular type of illness? Why is it appearing in this particular part of my body? What is it trying to tell me?"

Finding a meaningful connection between your

psyche and your body can help you to feel that you play a part in what is happening to you. Other questions you can ask yourself are: "Have I been living fully enough? Do I take a passive or even a negative stance toward my life? Do I simply react to people and situations, or do I initiate interaction and activity?"

Some people discover that they have been harboring a death wish; their illness is forcing them to choose between living or dying. It is helpful to examine through dream interpretation and/or use of the imagination whether you have unconsciously been hiding a wish to give up on life.

Sometimes you can find quite justifiable reasons for wanting to die. It is beneficial to examine the gains you might be getting from being sick, such as attention or a way out of a hateful situation. After identifying what you are accomplishing by being sick, you can select healthier ways of meeting your needs. In this way you become more aware of meaning and learn that action in itself can be meaningful. Life can feel empty without a sense of meaning.

☐ *Choice* Psychotherapy can help you to increase your awareness of your own experience, and as this happens, you will discover that every minute of every day you are making choices. It seems that first you have to realize that, yes, you can wipe out your existence in many different ways and that you have *chosen* not to take such action. Once you realize that you are free to die, you also realize that you are choosing to live. Choice is a supreme power.

In many people's minds, cancer is so synonymous with death that the awareness of the possibility of choice is often startling. I remember one client, Hillary, coming to me the same day she had been told that she had a malignant tumor in her rectum and that it was imperative she have a colostomy immediately. She was terrified. During our session I brought up the subject of choice. She looked at me with great relief and gratitude and said, "You know, I'd completely forgotten that I had any choice in this whatsoever!" Then she began to sob, saying that the tears were not so much over the diagnosis as they were for the humiliation she felt at having her body completely taken over by someone else. The realization that these choices were really hers to make gave her reassurance and dignity.

Choice usually involves giving up some form of dependence on authority and assuming responsibility for making independent decisions, in particular, decisions about the direction of your health. Psychotherapy can help you to believe in yourself and your right to make your own decisions. You need help to stand up to the sometimes overbearing authority of the medical establishment, to demand what is right for you and in your best interest.

You are free to choose a doctor whom you like and with whom you feel comfortable. You are free to obtain as many opinions as you like. You can choose to change doctors. You can choose the type of treatment that you believe will help you the most. You can say *no* to certain treatments. You can refuse medication.

You can choose to ask for help. You can choose to be involved in psychotherapy, and you can also choose alternative methods of therapy. You can choose to do more with your life, to pursue a healthier lifestyle, to develop closer friendships, and to improve your relations with your family. You can choose your attitude to your illness. You can choose to live and to bring more meaning and joy into your life. The choices are yours.

☐ *Will* Will is a direct expression of yourself. Will is action. It has been described as "an intelligent energy, directed toward a definite aim, having a purpose." The crisis of illness, and the struggle between moving toward illness or health, can put you in touch with an inner energy or power, an experience of "willing."

Some of my clients have a much stronger desire to live than others, and this desire appears to increase the resistance of the body to stress and disease. By helping to mobilize your will to live, you are building your health; you are also working toward the unfolding of your soul or essential being.

Because it nourishes the dynamic principle of self, the process of psychotherapy can help inspire the will to live. We all need to share our dreams, fantasies, and desires, to explore our interests and hobbies, to discover our unique attributes, and to learn how to value ourselves.

Psychotherapy can lead your will in the direction of challenge and the setting up of goals. Meeting challenges and having goals help to create purpose in living and a spirit of hope, intention, and optimism. They help translate the will to live into a physical reality. This stage of mobilizing the will to live is crucial, because it activates the transformation of insight into action. Norman Cousins describes the will to live as a window on the future. It opens you up to such help as the world has to offer, and it connects that help to your body's own resources for fighting disease. Cousins calls this process the "chemistry" of the will to live.

He hypothesizes that positive emotions such as hope, faith, laughter, and the will to live can produce positive chemical changes within the body. I agree with his hypothesis and believe that this concept is partially responsible for the health of the people described in this book.

☐ *Responsibility* At this stage of psychotherapy, you will have already integrated the concept of responsibility to some degree through your exploration of awareness, meaning, and choice. By now you will be more open to the suggestion that perhaps, knowingly or unknowingly, you have played a part in becoming sick. With this acceptance comes the readiness to take responsibility for becoming well.

At this point some individuals opt for feeling guilty for getting sick. Guilt, however, will only reinforce the already existing lack of self-esteem. You need to remember that you can choose whether to feel guilty or not. You can overcome guilt by understanding that illness can be the result of unconscious motivation. Once you are aware of your involvement in this process, you can change it. You may also be getting sick to meet a very real need, such as a need for attention, and again, once you are aware of what you are doing, you can meet your needs in a healthier way. You can confront your guilt and strive for more honesty and thus responsibility for yourself and your relationships.

To accept responsibility does not imply an acceptance of guilt. To choose to feel guilty is to choose a negative, passive, and apathetic stance. The action of taking responsibility is, conversely, positive and energetic. Instead of feeling guilty, you can find excitement in learning how to translate intellectual willingness into life-affirming action.

You can change your line of questioning from "Why me?" to "Why not me?" With this change, the responsibility for the answer to this question is placed on yourself rather than on an external authority.

Have you been resisting change? Fear of change is often a stumbling block. Therapy can help you to understand this fear and move toward a metamorphosis.

Becoming involved in psychotherapy is a form of

taking responsibility. It gives you an opportunity to explore your unconscious and discover if negative, destructive forces have been influencing you. For example, one of my clients, Nancy, uncovered a lifelong script, learned from her family, which repeated, "What's the use?" She was continually feeling fearful and defeated. Once she uncovered this hindrance, she worked toward developing a new script for herself.

Taking responsibility for your fear of death can lead you toward a different perspective and help you to see that perhaps you have actually been afraid to live!

Learning to be responsible for taking better care of yourself requires making significant changes in your lifestyle.

☐ *Strategies:* Psychotherapy can help you to discover strategies for promoting your health and happiness and help you to accept responsibility for maintaining this changed, innovative, and nourishing style of life.

You need to tailor strategies to suit your particular tastes and meet your individual needs. For example, decide whether you prefer to work with a group or on your own, whether you like outdoor or indoor activities; perhaps a combination of such strategies will seem best. Select what you would like to do and do it your way.

All of the people I have worked with stated their need to become more active physically. Most of them acknowledged their need to become a part of something larger than themselves. Different individuals filled this need in different ways: through marathon running, through closer communion with nature, through identification with a religious or spiritual group, through a realization that they were part of what Jung called the "collective unconscious."

Most became involved in psychotherapy.

All found humor effective.

Most felt the need to set goals and create challenge and purpose in their lives. Hans Selye and Gregory Bateson each produced a book.

Almost everyone practiced some sort of imagery or visualization. Visualization can help you to experience your power, to see that you have the potential to effect change; it can help you to mobilize your own resources for self-realization and health.

You need to discover ways to encourage your general health. These could include taking regular vacations, breathing pollution-free air, drinking pure water, finding time for silence and meditation, participating in the arts and aesthetic activities. Creative expression in any form can be health giving.

Strategies of this kind can be a way of demonstrating, to yourself and to the world around you, your beliefs and your affirmation of and joy in living. Strategies are vehicles whereby you can give expression to meaning, purpose, values, and aspirations. Your strategies reveal your will to live.

☐ *Change:* As you become more aware of yourself and learn how to express yourself more completely, you will notice that you are beginning to change. Your therapist will notice you changing and reinforce your strengths. He or she will encourage the positive, loving, and alive parts of your personality. Change may occur in many dimensions: change in feelings, change in jobs or profession, change in personal relationships and, most noticeably, change in attitudes and values.

It is in the process of therapy that the life force of the sick person can be touched. The ill people I have worked with appeared to be out of touch with their bodies, their emotions, and their spirits. It seemed wise, then, to engage their intellectual processes in searching for health. This meant talking about values, concepts, ideas, ultimate realities, discussing whatever was important to them. Once the life force is engaged, you become more aware of your body and how you feel.

When you are feeling hopeless, you need direction, honesty, and empathy from a strong therapist who is willing to share his or her own feelings about health and disease, living and dying. Your therapist can help you to explore, expand, and create meaning in your life, to open doors of which you were unaware.

The most important facet of the therapeutic process is the human encounter between yourself and your therapist. Be sure to interview several therapists before choosing one. If you are sick, you may be feeling lost and in despair. Despair has been described as an egg in a no-win situation. If a rock drops on the egg—poor egg. If the egg drops on a rock—poor egg. It is imperative that at some point you feel and relate to the vitality, caring, and spirit of your therapist, that the process involves a giving and receiving of these priceless gifts.

Psychotherapy can ignite the life force that lies within you. A therapist's empathic understanding, care, education and encouragement could provide the first stepping stones to a changed, life-affirming stance. As you experience your existence in relationship to your therapist, you can uncover a pathway to the meaning of your existence, the meaning of your life.

☐ *MASSAGE*

Massage is an ancient healing art. Long before Christ was born, massage was used to relieve pain. The art of massage is believed to have originated in China and to have developed from folk medicine. Numerous references to massage can be found in the medical literature of ancient Egypt, Persia, and Japan. In the West this healing art has been used since the birth of civilization—the ancient Greek physicians Hippocrates and Asclepius proclaimed the benefits of massage. More recently, Sweden, Germany, Austria, and France became strong advocates of massage, and today England and North America are making their contributions to this important field.

The key message of massage lies in the form of communication itself. It is given without words. There is a mind-body-spirit exchange between you and your massage therapist. You are the receiver, but you play a part in the way your massage is received.

Among the physiological benefits of massage are improved circulation (massage facilitates venous and lymphatic flow); an increased flow of nutrients to the muscles, facilitated by improved circulation and relaxation of muscle fibers; the release and elimination of wastes and toxins from tense muscles; improved muscle tone and improved functioning of the muscular system; and a reduction of certain types of edema.

We know that stiffness and physical tension are caused not only by physical activity but are often directly related to our mental and emotional experience. Think of a garden hose, full of water, with a knot in it. Tension experienced years ago, as well as daily, becomes lodged in our bodies, blocking the flow of energy. This dammed-up tension inhibits the full expression of our selves.

One of the more subtle effects of massage follows from making the commitment to take the time and money to make an appointment, keep it, and let yourself give in to this healthy, healing way. This act can boost your self-esteem and your confidence.

We have recent proof that therapeutic touch, or the laying on of hands, is a uniquely effective human act. In a controlled experiment, a group of people were touched with the intent of helping or healing. They reported feeling an unusual heat from the toucher's hand. They also showed significant measurable changes in hemoglobin values. They reported feeling profoundly relaxed and experiencing a sense of well-being.

Touch, particularly as it is applied through massage, can make an important contribution to healing.

Develop a lifestyle that includes regular massage. Through massage, you will learn to respect and appreciate the magnificence of your body, and this positive attitude toward yourself will help you move toward greater health and vitality.

☐ HOW TO GIVE YOURSELF A MASSAGE*

Assume a comfortable position, standing, kneeling, or sitting. Close your eyes and relax your body. Take some long, deep breaths and wait until you feel calm and centered.

☐ *Head:* Raise your arms over your head, shaping each hand as if you were holding a tennis ball. Keeping your fingers curved and firm, begin to tap your head all over. Move from the top of your head downward in all directions. Do this for at least a minute, ending at the back of your neck. Be aware of any change in feeling in your head. This stimulation

---

*The Self-Health Guide, Kripalu Yoga Fellowship, 1980.

is good for your head, spine, and sinuses; when directed to the center top of the head, it may help relieve hemorrhoids.

☐ *Ears:* Gently pinch the lobes of your ears. Put your thumbs on the front and your fingers on the back of your ears. Pinch and pull your fingers away from three points: top, center, and lower lobe. This is beneficial for both the kidneys and the intestines. Rub the skin in front of your ears up and down until you feel heat. This is good for your small intestines.

☐ *Forehead:* Place one hand in the other, with the back of the right hand in the palm of the left, bring them to rest lightly on your forehead. Keeping your hands still, gently turn your head from side to side so that it receives a gentle massage. Speed up slightly, then slow down again before stopping. This is very beneficial for your liver.

☐ *Nose:* Pinch the bridge of your nose firmly, hold for a minute, then rub. This is good for your sinuses and your heart. Also pinch and massage your upper lip.

☐ *Temples:* Rub your temples in a circular motion with three fingers to alleviate general tension.

☐ *Eyes:* With two fingers of each hand, press gently all around the bony sockets of your eyes. Then cover them lightly for a short time and watch your inner sky.

☐ *Cheeks:* Pat your cheeks with your fingers to stimulate your lungs. Then tap vigorously all along your cheekbones, starting at your nose, out and down in front of your ears to the angle of your jaw. This is good for your large intestine and sinuses and can sometimes help to relieve depression.

☐ *Jaw:* With thumbs hooked under your jaw at its outside edge, and fingers on top, press in small circles toward the center. This helps to relieve headaches and tension in your jaw and is good for your gums and teeth.

☐ *Mouth:* Tap and massage your lips and all around your mouth. Stretch your mouth open and make sounds. Move your jaw from side to side with your mouth wide open. This helps to relieve tension.

Pause for a minute to shake out your hands and to take a few deep breaths. Notice how you are feeling.

☐ *Neck and Shoulders:* Make your right hand into a loose fist, bring it across your chest, and pound vigorously down the left side of your neck and out to the tip of your shoulder. Support your right elbow in your left hand as you do this. Reach around to the back of your shoulder and pound your upper back muscle. You hold a great deal of tension there. Reverse hands and do the same for your right neck and shoulder. This stimulates your eliminative process, particularly in your large intestine.

☐ *Arms:* Make your right hand into a fist with the upper parts of your fingers flat on your palms and pound down the inside of your left arm to stimulate your heart and lungs. Then pound up the outside to stimulate the large and small intestines and regulate body heat. Do this several times, and then reverse arms and repeat.

☐ *Chest:* Take both hands and pound the center of your upper chest at your collarbone, moving out beneath it to your shoulders, making a deep AAAH-HHHH sound as you do so. This helps you to release tension and to open up your lungs. It is particularly good if you have a cough. Then pound down the center of your upper body and out along the bottom edges of your rib cage. Here you could use your fingertips and tap more gently because you are working with your liver, spleen, and stomach.

☐ *Intestines:* Gently pound your lower abdomen and pelvic area in clockwise circles (up the right side, across the top, and down the left) following the path of the colon.

Pause again and shake out your hands. Sit with your eyes closed for a moment and feel the energy moving in your body.

☐ *Thighs:* Pound vigorously down your thighs from pelvis to knee in three lines: center, inside, and outside. This is good for all your inner organs.

☐ *Lower Back and Buttocks:* Lean forward, then pound your lower back on either side of your spine down into your buttocks, ending at the small depressions. This is highly beneficial for your sciatic nerve and for your whole lower-back area. It is also good for your eliminative organs and your kidneys.

☐ *Legs:* Now stretch out your legs and gently thump them up and down, releasing at your knees. This helps to relieve cramps and tension.

☐ *Feet:* Lift up one foot and, with the knee bent, shake it out. Rotate your foot around your ankle. While holding the knee with the same-side hand, take the opposite hand and pinch the back of the ankle, releasing any tension in the ankle joint. Place your foot, sole up, on your opposite thigh and begin to pound vigorously up and down on the sole of your foot. Repeat with the other foot. This stimulates the whole body, because the soles of the feet contain reflex points which connect to all the organs of your body.

Now put your thumbs one on top of the other for strength, and press them along the sole of one foot in four lines from your heels to your toes. One line will follow the inside edge of your foot, two will be in the middle, and the fourth will be along the very outside edge. Rotate your toes one by one, starting with the big toe. Then press each toe back toward the sole of the foot, then out toward the front of the leg, before snapping your fingers off sharply at the end of each toe. Repeat with the other foot.

☐ *Hands:* Finally, give your caring hands a good massage. They have accomplished some very beneficial work! First, shake them out to remove static energy and fatigue. Then, taking one finger at a time, rotate and twist each with the whole of your other hand, bending it back and forth as you did your toes. Pull your fingers, cracking your knuckles if you can, as this loosens the joints by redistributing your synovial fluid, a thick, colorless lubricating fluid. Massage the palm of each hand with your fingers and thumb. This is good for your heart.

Bite (gently!) the end of your little fingers at the point just to the outside of center near the top of your nail. This is good for your heart. Massage deeply the webbed area between your thumb and first finger. There are pressure points here for your sinuses and intestines. Massaging this area can also help headaches, constipation and menstrual cramps. Shake out your hands.

Sit quietly, with your eyes closed, and become aware of your breathing. Feel the energy moving in your body. How do you feel different? Be aware that *you* have refreshed and re-energized yourself. Remember to give this gift to yourself when you are feeling tense or tired.

☐ CREATIVE AND AESTHETIC GROWTH

Creativity, the ability to explore, imagine, and invent, is an instinct we all possess. We are born with it. We use it to solve our problems in life and to express ourselves uniquely, to document ourselves. Professor of psychology and author Carl Rogers has suggested that creativity is an end in itself, that people are creative to the extent that they fulfill their potentialities as human beings. He equates the mainspring of creativity—our longing for self-actualization—with the curative force of psychotherapy. He describes this force as the urge to expand, extend, develop, and mature.

Certainly, many intermediate steps lie between this innate capacity for self-expression and more complex forms of creation. A certain degree of emotional freedom is necessary for any kind of creative expression. For many of us, this emotional freedom has been curtailed or blocked by family, teachers, and other well-meaning members of society. It remains buried under layers of psychological defenses: its existence may even be denied. I share with Rogers, however, the belief that each of us possesses this creative ability and only needs support and encouragement for its release and expression.

The repercussions of nonexpression can be great. Sometimes the damming up of this emotional and creative flow manifests itself in illness. Many of my clients have forgotten that this ability is inherent within themselves. It has been extremely important in their recovery to reclaim this ability—this fountain of life.

Mary Jean Champ, described in Chapter 11, rediscovered through therapy her ability to paint. When she paints, she feels alive: she is expressing her life force. We are both absolutely convinced that as long as she continues to express her *self* through painting, her cancer will not dare to reappear.

Our aesthetic understanding—our notions of truth, goodness, and beauty—informs and structures our experience of ourselves and the world. Creative activity generates aesthetic growth, and aesthetic growth engenders creativity. The educator Herbert Read has described this process as

> . . . the education of the senses upon which consciousness, and ultimately the intelligence and judgment of the individual are based. It is only in so far as these senses are brought into harmonious and habitual relationship with the external world that an integrated personality is built up. Without such integration we get not only the psychologically unbalanced types familiar to those in the helping professions, but what is even more disastrous from the point of view of the general good, those arbitrary systems of thought, dogmatic or rationalistic in origin, which seek in spite of the natural facts to impose a logical or intellectual pattern on the work of organic life. This adjustment of the senses to their ob-

jective environment is perhaps the most important function of aesthetic education.

Aesthetic growth is thus essential for clear and unobstructed thinking, feeling, and perceiving and for their expression and assimilation.

It is important for your health to receive as well as express aesthetic forms of communication. There is a multitude of art forms that you can use to help heal yourself: the visual arts, the performing arts, the literary arts—all offer enlightenment and inspiration. Time spent in beautiful, natural surroundings offers another form of aesthetic experience.

I have found music, in particular, to be a wonderful healer. I recommend that you listen to music that supports you rather than makes demands of you. Find selections that help you to feel peaceful. Look for music that has a regular rhythm, with a tempo similar to your resting heartbeat. Don't choose music with extremes of dynamics or pitch. Search for a melodic line with restful movement, and consonant rather than disconsonant chord progressions.

Some of my favorites are: Debussy's "Claire de Lune"; Pachelbel's Canon in D; Haydn's Cello Concerto in C; Bach's Air on a G String from Suite no. 3, BWV 1068, the Harpsichord Concerto in F minor, BWV 1056 (Largo), and the Concerto for Two Violins in D minor (the second movement); Vaughan Williams's *Fantasy on a Theme by Thomas Tallis*; Barber's Adagio for Strings from Quartet, op. 11; Elgar's Enigma Variations no. 9 called "Nimrod" and no. 13 "Romanza"; and "Beim Schlafengehn," the third of Richard Strauss's *Four Last Songs*. Last, but by no means least, are Mozart's piano concertos no. 22 (K482), in E-flat major, no. 17 (KV453) in G major, and no. 21 (KV467) in C major. I also love Mozart's Symphony no. 40 (KV550) in G minor.

By listening to selections such as the above, you

will discover that you can lower your heart rate, decrease your blood pressure, and reduce pain and anxiety. You may also find that you have less need for medication. You will be able to induce contentment, relaxation, happiness, and peace of mind.

Make your own tapes, invest in a tape recorder, and take your music with you. If music be the food of life, play on!

☐ SPIRITUALITY

Lack of spiritual development can play a definitive role in the development of illness. This was demonstrated by some of those interviewed for this book, and by many of my clients. Most of us are unaware that this dimension is lacking from our lives until some experience demands that we wake up. Including this dimension in your life is like standing in the sunshine instead of the shade, having your curtains open instead of drawn, opening your eyes wide to the life force around you instead of defending yourself against it.

By spiritual development I mean any activity that lifts your spirit, expands your awareness, or purges your soul. The concepts of soul or spirit have received many different interpretations; the essence of these concepts is hard to capture in words. It has been my experience that after seeing an excellent ballet, film, or play, or a particularly fine piece of sculpture or painting, I feel astonishingly nourished. I am happy, content, and peaceful, as if I have received a very special gift. This same feeling can happen while drifting in a canoe, standing under a waterfall or on top of a mountain, gazing at a flower or a newborn baby. My responses have included wonder, surprise, awe, and joy, and it is this kind of experience that I call spiritual. Such an event takes you out of yourself and leaves you feeling more complete, whole, connected with the universe, and in some way changed.

Some have named this form of experience "transpersonal;" some describe it as touching your "higher power," or "superconscious." "Transpersonal" means going beyond, or surpassing, the personal or individual. Roberto Assagioli defined the "superconscious" as that region of the mind from which "we receive our higher intuitions and inspirations—artistic, philosophical, or scientific 'ethical imperatives' and urges to humanitarian and heroic action. It is the source of the higher feelings, such as altruistic love or genius and of the states of contemplation, illumination, and ecstasy. In this realm are latent the higher psychic functions and spiritual energies." Abraham Maslow called this form of experience a "peak experience" and believed it had a role in the development of spiritual values.

These kinds of experiences include a feeling of universality or connectedness; they are the stimuli at the heart of much social and artistic action. By allowing this spiritual dimension to enter your life, you can reap rich benefits: a fresh perspective on life, an expanded perception of reality, the healing of past trauma and hurt, the evocation of a vital and healing energy, inner guidance, an improved self-image, a clearer sense of identity, and new meaning and value in your life.

Becoming aware of your spiritual life will help you to expand your consciousness of self in relation to the world. Rollo May has said that the more consciousness you have of yourself, the more spontaneous and creative you can be—because consciousness of self actually expands your control of your life, and with that expanded power comes the capacity to let yourself go. By letting go, you are better able to experience who you really are and to give yourself permission to develop and actualize who you might become.

☐ Imagery Exercise for Wholeness

The following imagery exercise (adapted from "Embracing Disease" by Vivian King) will help you to experience the thread of consciousness that connects your energy to that of the whole universe. It demonstrates the relationship of each unit of your life energy to the cosmic energy that orders the world.

Have a friend read the following instructions to you slowly, or read them into a tape recorder slowly so that when you do this exercise you will have the time to feel the experience.

Find yourself a quiet, comfortable place. Close your eyes and breathe deeply for a few minutes. Check your body for areas of tension. Gradually unwind and relax your muscles. Let your breathing return to normal.

Imagine yourself becoming very, very small. You finally become so tiny that you are not even perceived as a particle. Now imagine that you have entered a microscopic world and that you yourself are a unit of energy. You are in motion because of your relationship to other moving units of energy. You are moving very fast, and someone closely studying your movement would notice that you, along with the units of energy around you, form an atom.

Let yourself identify with the consciousness of this atom. You are an atom composed of many units of energy moving rapidly to create your atomic structure. Unbeknown to you, you are one atom among many comprising a molecule.

Identify with the consciousness of this molecule. You have a whole universe within you, a universe of atoms. You are the god or goddess of your atomic universe. What happens to you will directly affect each atom. As a molecule, you are unaware that you, along with many molecules, make up a cell.

Let yourself become this single cell. You are a cell with a universe of molecules within you. You are the god or goddess of this molecular universe. This universe depends upon you. As a cellular god or goddess, you also depend upon each molecule within you. What happens to each molecule affects you. Now, as a cell, become aware that you are one cell among many in a single muscle.

Remember to breathe naturally.

Identify with the consciousness of your muscle, one muscle with many cells working together. You are a god or goddess to the many cells that make up this muscle. As a muscle, you become aware that you are one muscle in a bundle of muscles and that you work with other muscle groups to form your heart.

Let yourself become your heart, rhythmically contracting and expanding as each muscle group works together to pump blood through your body. You are the god or goddess of this pulsating, pumping, rhythmic universe. This universe depends upon you. Become aware that you also depend upon each muscle, cell, molecule, atom, and unit of energy in this universe. If one group of your muscles is overworked or has insufficient oxygen, all your muscles will be affected. You are also aware that you depend upon the organs and systems of your body. You belong to a larger universe. You are the heart of a person. You!

You are a person with many systems, organs, muscles, bones, and blood vessels. You are a living universe, and your consciousness is the god or goddess of this universe. What you do, say, eat, feel, and think affects your universe. You are aware that you embody emotions and thoughts. You have a unique personality. As the god or goddess of this personal universe, become aware that you are one person among many people on earth. You are a part of the body of humanity.

Breathe normally.

The joys, sufferings, and problems of each person affect your whole body in some way. You are the body of humanity. You share the earth with the elements, with minerals, plants, and animals. Experience the planet Earth as one part of the solar system and identify with the consciousness of the god or goddess of the solar system, the solar god or goddess. Recognize that all your parts and aspects depend upon one another. Each planet directly affects each life on earth. Turbulence in one area will affect all other areas.

Then become aware that you are one solar system among billions. Your solar system is one small part of the cosmos. Reflect upon the cosmic consciousness of the Great Spirit.

Breathe deeply.

In the same way that you depend upon the god or goddess of the universe, the cells in your body depend upon you. Your goal then, is to become a wiser, more loving god or goddess to your internal universe for your own sake and for the sake of humanity.

Bcome aware of your breathing and gently bring your consciousness back to present time and space. Think of *dis-ease* as pain of evolution as we learn to be more responsive to the universe within.

☐ 16
REVITALIZATION

And the end of all our exploring
Will be to arrive where we started
And know the place for the first time.
—T. S. Eliot

You can revitalize your life force even though you are very sick, even dying. The experiences of the people portrayed in this book are the evidence. "Dying to live" may sound paradoxical, but life's meaning is often found within this paradox. The process is somewhat like spiral learning, which is the experience of confronting the same problem but handling it in a different way, because the next time you meet the problem, *you* will have changed. The words of T.S. Eliot given above capture the magic of this process.

This chapter is divided into four related areas: research, education, a paradigm for holistic health, and conclusions.

☐ RESEARCH

You have witnessed throughout this book personal testimonials describing the link between emotional distress and disease. You have also learned that emotional distress can weaken your ability to resist illness.

The fact that there is a connection between negative psychological factors (distress) and tumor growth has been well documented by scientific research. The psychological indicators include: (1) feelings of isolation, (2) inability to express negative emotions, (3) feelings of helplessness and despair, and (4) loss experienced preceding the diagnosis.

The prediagnostic psychological histories of the persons described in this book generally support the existing research. They have illustrated that for individuals suffering from cancer, the typical life-history pattern in childhood and/or adolescence is one marked by feelings of isolation, a conviction that meaningful relationships bring pain or rejection, and difficulty in expressing negative emotions. The fourth aspect of the pattern involves loss of an important emotional relationship followed by feelings of hopelessness and despair. Subsequent to this phase, the first symptoms of cancer usually appear.

Cancer patients appear to invest their energy in a relationship or vocation to the extent that it becomes their reason for living. When this role or relationship is removed, through a separating agent such as death, or retirement, or moving away, the result is despair. This despair is often associated with a loss suffered in childhood, a disaster whose repetition is continually anticipated, consciously or unconsciously.

Most of the people described in this book were very

much aware of the experience of loss. For them, loss extended far beyond the loss of a loved one: it included loss of communication, loss of challenge or will, loss of children, home, or parents, and loss of self and relationships.

My research confirms that of the Simontons, who found four outstanding differences between those cancer patients who die and those who outlive their terminal date. The survivors (1) assume some responsibility for their illness, (2) take a positive stance toward life, (3) believe they can exert some influence over the course of their disease, and (4) are able to mobilize a stronger will to live. These four characteristics make a considerable difference to the outcome of any illness, terminal or not. They are all attributes that can be developed through various forms of psychological intervention.

In response to their diagnoses, the individuals described in this book evolved in their thinking and feeling. They reassessed their values and beliefs, chose alternative strategies for addressing their disease, and developed more rewarding lifestyles. Their recoveries support the research that indicates a correlation between stress and the immune system. The evidence indicates that, by learning to understand their own stress levels, to handle stress effectively, and to understand and believe in their own immune systems, these people were gradually able to kill and flush away their cancer.

Glasser puts it this way: "To cure a disease, not just treat it, you must help (your) body do it itself. It is *your* body that is the hero, not science, not antibiotics, not machines or new devices .... It is *your* body, too, that must seek out that last single, hidden cancer cell, missed by radiation or chemotherapy, and destroy it if you are to survive." [Emphases mine].

Your body is endowed with natural recuperative

mechanisms called "homeostatic responses," natural processes that enable it to return to a normal state after a disturbance upsets equilibrium. The process that the individuals depicted in this book underwent was more than homeostatic. It was transformative:

> The development of scar tissue is not a truly homeostatic response; it makes the scarred part of the body better able to resist the insult that caused scarring. Recovery from a given infection is usually accompanied by persistent cellular changes that produce a lasting immunity to that particular infection. Persons who have lost a limb or become blind tend to develop compensatory skills that become part of their new personality. *Instead of being simply homeostatic, the response of the organism corresponds rather to a creative adaptation that is achieved by a permanent change in the body or the mind.* (Dubos, 1959, p.16) [Emphasis mine]

One of my clients, Jessie, expressed her experience with scar tissue in this way:

> Behind every storm is the sun, waiting to heal the wound; and each scar represents a truth learned. Scar tissue is strong, more durable and ready to carry on; I can take more risks and live life more fully if I allow myself. I look around and see others who have allowed scar tissue to become insensitive and hard, and they hide behind it. So, as always, *there is a choice and only I can make the choice for me.* I love my scar tissue: it gives me courage to carry on and grow. [Emphasis mine]

The experiences of the individuals I have written about support the results of a large body of research on how attitudes and belief systems, expectations or self-fulfilling prophesies, the placebo effect, biofeedback, and hope and optimism affect your health.

☐ EDUCATION

Norman Cousins has said: "Knowing more about the gift of life is not merely a way of satisfying random curiosity. In the end, it is what education is all about."

Personal Agency, or the Healing Path, is a process of education: it is a philosophy of living, a theory about how to live. The transformation of consciousness is an educative process. Unfortunately, many people have never questioned the meaning of their existence, and even people who are dying are often not able to answer this question to their own satisfaction.

The seven stages of Personal Agency could be introduced to the educational process at most levels. The essential self is an inner force, unique to each of us, and the deep source of our growth. The stages of Personal Agency are a means of uncovering and nourishing the self's potential. The existence and the importance of this drive to fulfill personal destiny need to be woven in many different colors and shapes throughout the tapestry of education.

As you will recall, one of the strategies used by many of the individuals whose stories form part of this book is visualization or mental imagery. I believe that this technique could be used to great effect in education. Mental imagery, which involves concentration, thought, imagination, and a progression of consciousness, can lead to remarkable mental, emotional, spiritual, and physiological change. A creative technique for growth, it has been called the silent language of communication.

Educators today would be wise to restore to the school arena the tradition of the Greeks, in which equal emphasis was given to the body and the mind.

We all need to learn and relearn the importance of caring for our bodies by exercising, maintaining good nutrition, and obtaining fresh air, enough rest, and emotional and spiritual nourishment. These are ways of loving and giving to ourselves. We need to learn the connection between health and happiness—between health and fulfillment—and to understand the importance of our immune system and the part we play in inhibiting or helping it function.

Disease, for many, may have its roots in the attitudes learned in school. The message I learned from my own experience of school was that it is more important to be right than to be curious or imaginative. Memorization was more important than meaning, regurgitation earned more marks than critical inquiry, and discipline was valued more highly than understanding. Too often in the past, the emphasis of education has been on book knowledge, on analytical, linear, left-brain thinking. Conformity and "proper" performance have been the attributes rewarded.

Our educational system has neglected our natural creativity and by so doing has arguably tampered with our health. Being creative is an essential part of human fulfillment. Self-realization implies self-knowledge, self-trust, and openness to the world. Education should surely be responsible for leading us to an awareness of the richness and depth of life and of our own capacities to participate in these mysteries. The search for self and the search for health merge and intertwine.

The critical question for education today is: What does humankind want for itself? Destruction or affirmation? Will humankind move against life or for life? Will we simply react to events, or will we initiate, take responsibility, and act creatively? Our future depends on which direction we choose. Educators have the opportunity to create an awareness of choice, will, and responsibility, the human freedom and potential upon which Personal Agency is based.

We all need help from time to time in developing a positive stance, in establishing our openness to and acceptance of whatever is life-affirming in nature, other people, and ourselves. Educators have a role to play in activating this imperative experience.

The opposite of this affirmative stance is despair, which is akin to helplessness. If helplessness is "learned" behavior, and I believe that it is, then it can be unlearned. Depressed individuals can learn to exert greater control over their environment and, by experiencing their effectiveness, dissipate their depression. People who see problems in a negative light can learn to see these same problems from a different perspective, in a different context with a more positive meaning. Your mind-body-spirit functions as a unit; from understanding this comes the knowledge that you have the power to influence and change your life.

Health is wholeness. We need to expand our traditional approach to education and educate the whole person, to develop not just the intellect but also attitudes, feelings, imagination, spirit, body, and the creative mind. We need education in the context of family, school, work, religion, environment, and planet; we need to learn that we are individuals in relation to each other, the larger community, the world, and the universe.

☐ A PARADIGM FOR HOLISTIC HEALTH

The practice of medicine in the twentieth century has been primarily mechanistic and mainly allopathic (combating disease by treatments that produce effects different from those producd by the disease; that is, the use of drugs to alleviate symptoms), with the result that we living, breathing human beings have felt dehumanized. The need for alternative approaches to health and disease, to diagnosis and healing, is glaring. Such a change may well require a challenge to the world of medicine similar to the one that Einstein, by introducing the person and subjectivity into the study of material events, brought to the world of Newtonian physics.

Medicine today persists in downplaying the importance of the person and hence the personality. Often, when a somatic disease reveals the influence of psychological factors, the latter are treated as secondary complications of the primary, physical pathology. If modern medicine is to continue to be considered responsible in its professed role, sensitivity to and awareness of the psychological makeup of the individual must be incorporated into its practice.

It is time to look beyond the symptoms to the context of disease. The psychosocial constellation of influence "has been consistently ignored by current medical practice and by most of scientific cancer research programs" (Booth, 1972).

The face of disease has changed in Western society from a visage of contagion to that of chronicity and degeneration. The technology of modern medicine, although brilliant in many areas such as the development of vaccines and surgical procedures, is failing in its treatment of this type of disease. The latter include arteriosclerosis, diabetes, hypertension, chronic bronchitis, duodenal ulcers, diverticulitis, and ulcerative colitis. This change in the countenance of disease demands a qualitatively different approach to health and medicine, a new point of view that respects the impact and interaction of mind, body, spirit, and environment.

We need a dramatic shift in our patterns of consciousness. The physics of this century are leading the way by breaking the image of a mechanistic world. "The discoveries of Planck and Einstein revealed that the so-called laws of classical physics are really statistical generalizations or statements of probability, *that there is no determinism, and that what had been considered inanimate nature is not the passive object it had appeared to be*" (Booth, 1953). [Emphasis mine]

Physicist Fritjof Capra has compared the organic, unified, spiritual vision of reality expressed in Eastern philosophy to the emerging paradigm of physics. He views this shift in paradigms as indicative of a merging of East and West, a rise in the feminine principle (after two thousand years of patriarchal society), the end of the fossil-fuel age—as a move away from the mechanistic world of Descartes and Newton to "a globally interconnected world in which biological, psychological, social and environmental phenomena are all interdependent."

We are rediscovering what the ancients already knew: that matter, indeed all form, does not exist in and of itself. The essence of life is relationship, fluctuation, and dynamic flow. Consciousness, which the Cartesian-Newtonians attempted to control *out* of their experiments, thereby separating mind from body—our selves from our essential nature—is the conundrum that holds the answer to the mind-body-spirit connection. We are paradoxical creatures, not mere biological machines. We have unlimited fields of consciousness.

At long last, the fact of consciousness has been introduced into scientific medical research. It has been demonstrated, on the basis of exact neurophysiological experiments, that the subject as a sciential and self-conscious entity is an integral part of biological dynamics. Who we are affects who and what we become, and vice versa—our consciousness is inseparable from our being:

> This theoretical analysis provided a concept of medicine that disposed of the old dichotomies of body and mind, of causalism and voluntarism, as effectively as modern physics has disposed of the dichotomy of mass and energy.... For the scientist used to working in terms of quantifiable physical data, the very word "subject" had the connotation "subjective." The concept of something existing only in the mind of the patient entailed an *a priori* prejudice that there could be no place for the "subject" in the world of objective data.... This report emphasizes the idea that the *personal predisposition* of the victim is the one and only *indispensable factor* of the disease, *determining* the contingencies of life that trigger the development of neoplasia in a certain organ at a certain time. The nature of some of those contingencies has been established as the result of the tremendous body of scientific knowledge accruing from the search for specific cause of the disease. Many physical and chemical agents are statistically correlated with neoplasia; but neither do they prove carcinogenic for individuals equally exposed, nor is the timing of the disease explained by the physical facts. (Booth, 1979) [Emphases mine]

At the heart of a new paradigm of humanness must necessarily be the concept that, in our consciousness—both individual and collective—we do most certainly affect our health, our physical, mental, and spiritual being. The participants in this book are evidence to this fact. People must not be treated as if they were isolated, autonomous, mechanical units. We are "parts of nature, of wide communication networks, with preverbal and verbal channels" (Siirala, 1981). We inform our world, even as it informs us.

This wide communication network needs to be understood in a nonlinear framework. The modern-day theories of physics and chemistry provide just such a framework through which the ways whereby we participate in our own becoming can now be understood. For example, Ilya Prigogine's idea of dissipative structures, which won the 1977 Nobel Prize for chemistry, illustrates the link between biology and physics relative to ourselves.

Prigogine's theory describes an upward spiral movement toward higher orders—a process of becoming. At a fundamental level in nature, nothing is fixed; the patterns and organization of life are in constant motion. We living creatures are open systems involved in a continuous exchange of energy with our environment. Prigogine's term for open systems is "dissipative structures," by which he means forms or structures maintained by a continuous consumption of energy. Human beings are dissipative structures, highly organized and always in process. The more complex our structure, the more energy we require to maintain our connections. These connections are sustained by the flow of energy, and therefore our systems are always in flux. Increased complexity means increased energy demands—and a consequent increase in the system's instability. Prigogine has shown mathematically that this dissipation of energy creates the potential for sudden re-ordering. The continuous fluctuations of being shake up our systems, and elements of old patterns intersect in different ways and make new connections. The elements reorganize into a new whole. Our systems evolve. We are becoming.

For the individuals interviewed for this book a terminal diagnosis was the "shake-up"—the catalyst for their revitalization, for growth leading to the transformation and renewal of life. We do not have to accept a fate of predicted hopelessness; we can shape our own lives. Jung himself said that it was only after his own illness that he understood how important it is to affirm one's own destiny.

Our human nature is like that of clay: we have the capacity to be plastic and to be hard; to absorb energy and to store it; we have the ability to reproduce ourselves. The onus is on us to redefine life as we know it.

We are multidimensional beings: we need an approach to health that can help us to find harmony within ourselves and with our environment. We need a dynamic, interactive, holistic concept of health care that would combine technological treatment with a knowledge of and respect for our consciousness and its mind-body-spirit interrelations. Under this mandate, health care professionals would strive to provide services that would reflect and reinforce the unity of our physiological and psychological needs. This would involve teaching attitudes that affirm life and strategies for a revitalized mode of being—the foundations of Personal Agency.

Essential to the achievement of this goal is the recognition that the symptoms of illness are our allies. The current perception that symptoms are negative indicators belies the life-affirming nature of these messages—the communication that our individuality is due for a change. Illness is the result of the way we interact with our environment. Each one of us develops our own unique way of becoming sick and becoming well, of dying or living. Illness is the voice of conflict, showing us that some part of our life is out of whack, that disharmony exists, that something is not right. Listen to the voice of your illness.

New perspectives engender change, and illness seen from a more positive point of view can create opportunity. A confrontation with illness can mobilize your resources for healing; most important, it can inspire a dramatic shift in values. Illness is potentially transformative. For the individuals described in this book, the revelation or awareness created by their illness enabled them to break free into the uncertain and exciting world of growth and change. Their illness forced their awareness. "The hurting body forces us to remember that the body is the temple. Sickness—even cancer—is an invitation to re-enter the temple in search of our connection to what is beyond constricted consciousness" (Lockhart, 1977).

Having learned that we affect our health, the next step is to learn that living and dying are dynamic processes. We need to learn to confront the process of disease, accept it, and learn from it. If we can understand that we play an active, though sometimes unwitting role in getting sick, we are then obliged to participate in getting well. Life is a struggle between our creative, productive forces and our negative, destructive forces. The substance of this struggle involves growth, adaptation, interaction, and evolution. Health is not a state that can be purchased from medicine; health is struggle and change. In *Mirage of Health*, René Dubos described this concept well:

> In the world of reality, places change and man changes. Furthermore, his self-imposed striving for ever-distant goals makes his fate even more unpredictable than that of other living things. For this reason, health and happiness cannot be absolute and permanent values, however careful the social and medical planning. Biological success in all its manifestations is a measure of fitness, and fitness requires never-ending efforts of adaptation to the total environment, which is ever changing.
> ....Whereas other living things survive through adaptive changes, in their bodies and in their instincts, man strives to impose his own directional will on the relations that he has with the rest of the world. Consciously ... he decides on the kind of life he wishes to have; then *he acts* to render possible this way of life by *shaping* the environment and even attempting to *alter his own physical and mental self*. [Emphases mine]

For the paradigm of health to shift, our disease-care system must change to a health care system. In such a system, noninvasive forms of intervention such as the use of imagery, exercise, nutrition, meditation, psychotherapy, physiotherapy, naturopathy, massage, communion with nature, and identification with a larger power will replace the current emphasis on drugs and surgery. Professionals will be regarded as partners rather than supreme authorities. Qualitative information will be equally or more important than quantitative information. Most important of all, the process of health—the mind-body-spirit interaction—will become the focus of attention.

The foundations of a dynamic, interactive, holistic health paradigm will be an affirmative stance in life, a regard for illness as a metaphor for change, an acceptance that health and disease are dynamic life processes, an awareness of our individual potential for growth and change, and a belief in the correspondence between ourselves and our environment.

☐ CONCLUSIONS

As a race we have always grappled with the mysteries of life and death. Compare this struggle to that of the hero in ancient myth who, alone in the face of destiny, confronts and confirms our humanity and, in so doing, transforms him or herself. From behind thousands of faces, the single hero emerges as the archetype for humankind. "The prime function of mythology and rite ... has been to supply the symbols that *carry the human spirit* forward, in counteraction to those other constant human fantasies that tend to tie it back ... the purpose and actual effect of these [rituals] was to conduct people across those difficult thresholds of transformation that *demand a change* in the patterns not only of conscious but also of unconscious life" (Campbell, 1949). [Emphasis mine]

A type of hero has emerged in this book. The individuals whose stories are related here are hero participants and clients who developed innovative, successful strategies and new beliefs and values in the face of daunting odds. They, too, have carried their spirit forward and have transformed a diagnosis of death into a revitalization of themselves and their relationships. They chose to change their attitudes and old patterns of behavior, to release themselves from their pasts, and, in a sense, to be reborn into the future. Like the archetype of myth, they, too, crossed a threshold of transformation.

The journey of the hero is threefold: a separation from the world, a penetration to some sort of power, and a life-enhancing return. My participants and clients separated themselves from their routine life by re-examining the meaning of their lives and their values in life. They found their power by mobilizing their will to live, and they returned to life by developing survival strategies and by manifesting their renewal in creative, productive activity.

The power, agency, and creativity that I believe to be inherent in each one of us is brilliantly described in the following paragraph:

> [Man has the] unique power to remold his patterns of thought and behavior—to meet critical challenges by creative responses. And thus we have come full circle through biological evolution back to the various manifestations of human creativity, based on the undoing-redoing pattern which runs as a *leit-motif* from paedomorphosis to the revolutionary turning points in science and art: to the mental regeneration at which the regressive techniques of psychotherapy are aimed; and finally to the archetypes of death-and-

resurrection, withdrawal-and-return which recur in all mythologies. (Koestler, 1978)

Most of the individuals interviewed for this study mentioned that, as they struggled with the predicament of a terminal diagnosis, they became aware that they had somehow lost touch with a larger power or unity. They were referring to their loss of identification with such communal phenomena as nature, aesthetic experience, and various manifestations of God or a larger power—the collective unconscious, universal characteristics of human beings, the transpersonal self, or cosmic consciousness. Re-integration with these universals was part of their movement toward health.

The importance of the development of personality in our evolution must be emphasized. The developed human being has "crossed the threshold of self-consciousness to a new mode of thought, and as a result has achieved some degree of conscious integration—integration of the self with the outer world of men and nature, integration of the separate elements of the self with each other" (Huxley, 1959, p.19).

The appearance of this kind of human personality is: "the culmination of two major evolutionary trends—the trend toward more extreme individuation, and that toward more extensive interrelation and cooperation: persons are individuals who *transcend* their merely organic individuality in *conscious* participation" (ibid., p.20). [Emphases mine]

The potential for self-transformation and transcendence was realized by the six people interviewed for this study and by many of my clients.

Eight years have passed since the interviews upon which this book is based took place, and since that time four of the individuals interviewed have died.

When I interviewed Gregory Bateson, he seemed tired and disillusioned, but satisfied that he had completed his book. He lacked the desire to create new meaning or change in his life. He seemed ready to accept death. He died, at the age of seventy-six, of respiratory disorders.

Jim Searle did not come to terms with his mortality or resolve his feelings of guilt. He did not take time to explore himself or his relationships in depth. He seemed to be on the run both physically and psychologically, and his cancer continued to recur. It eventually killed him.

Ann Latimer never fully accepted her diagnosis. She avoided confronting her death and realized too late that her negativity, fierce independence, and unrelenting anger were not in her best interests. She, too, died of cancer.

Hans Selye followed his code of behavior, living actively and fully, eight years longer than expected. He died of a heart attack.

These four remarkable people progressed through the stages of the Healing Path, beat the odds, extended their lives, and improved greatly the quality of time they did live.

The other two participants in this study, Doug Scott and Dean Bishop, are both alive and healthy, with no sign of cancer, living active and productive lives.

You, too, have the inherent ability to reorganize and change yourself, to evolve into a different, more harmonious state of being, of dynamic interaction within yourself and with other people.

"Self-organization" has been described as the central, dynamic principle of life that gives rise to self-healing, self-renewal, adaptation, and self-transcendence—to development, learning, and evolution. The meaning of the term "self-organization" is similar to the meaning of Personal Agency. The people interviewed for this book became "self-organizers."

I have been profoundly affected by the people I interviewed, as well as by my clients. Their courage to become and to live more fully has had a strong impact on my own growth. They inspired me to accept challenge, anxiety, stress, and pleasure in ways I had not yet experienced.

The theologian Paul Tillich described courage as "confronting anxiety, resisting despair, and facing the void." These six people did just that, and their responses resulted in the revitalization of their lives.

I was deeply impressed with the totality and variation of change that I observed within my clients and the individuals I interviewed: the changes they effected encompassed the psychological, physical, and spiritual. There was an overall transformation of consciousness. Due to the intimate nature of the interview and of therapy, I was able to observe the multifaceted unity of each person. This unity reminded me of a prism in that the facets or dimensions were separate, related, and emanated from a powerful center. I sensed a deep inner force within each one. Each person chose his or her own unique path for fulfillment and change, one that suited individual purposes, needs, and spirit.

I believe in the concept of "healing through meeting," described by Martin Buber. I have often felt this to be the true essence of psychotherapy. Once a person has had the experience of being "met"—of being confirmed or empowered through meeting—a trust, meaning, or significance in living is created. It was, therefore, interesting for me to find that each of the individuals interviewed had at some time met a "significant other" during the course of their lives. This "significant other" was usually a friend, grandparent, minister, teacher, or therapist who believed in them, had faith in them, and let them know this belief. It is difficult to have faith in yourself if you have never experienced someone else believing in you. Mutual trust is a prerequisite for growth.

Toward the conclusion of the writing of this book I was asked by a minister if I had included a section on faith healing. I realized then that my whole book is based on faith, but faith of a different genre.

Faith healing generally occurs when people place the responsibility for their healing in someone other than themselves: a doctor, minister, cultist, or shaman. The essence of my belief is that healing is the result of a faith that emanates from within ourselves. This is a faith that aspires to increased consciousness and awareness. This kind of faith resonates throughout my book: my faith in the positive dimensions of human nature, the faith of the participants and my clients in their ability to heal themselves, their faith in me and my research, my faith in psychotherapy and education as rejuvenating vehicles, my faith in myself to accomplish this book, our faith in life, death, and rejuvenation.

The search for health, the search for life, the discovery of the changes we need to make in order to live are all based on a faith inspired by the beauty and wonder of and reverence for nature, life, and spirit.

☐ Appendix

This Appendix describes the methods used to analyze the data generated by taped and transcribed interviews.

The sources used in devising a method for analyzing this information were Glaser and Strauss(1967) and Glaser (1978).

Glaser and Strauss were chosen because of their belief that theory is discovered from data systematically obtained and analyzed. They call this "grounded theory," meaning that information and understanding can emerge from the data if one allows the data source, the interviews, to provide what is relevant and meaningful for the event being studied.

Their method for achieving this is called "the constant comparative method." It includes, first, a comparison of incident with incident for the purpose of establishing the underlying pattern and its variations, which then become the generated concepts and hypotheses. Second, the concepts are compared to more incidents generating new theoretical properties of the concepts and more hypotheses. Third, the concepts are compared with each other for the purpose of establishing the best synthesis for description and integration. Thus, the concepts and hypotheses that will eventually form the theory emerge from the data. My theory for this study is grounded in the research interviews and in the expressed experience of the participants.

☐ THE ANALYSIS: PHASE ONE

There were two distinct phases in the data analysis. The purpose of the first phase was to develop and organize individual descriptions of the participants, which would then be presented to them for their interest and validation. The following is the seven-step procedure designed to develop an individual description of the experience of each person interviewed.

☐ *Step 1—The Setting:* The tape-recorded interview was transcribed verbatim with all the statements of both the participant and interviewer. The tape recording was also on hand to clarify by sound and inflection any vagueness of meaning.

☐ *Step 2—Identification and Enumeration of Incidents:* The analysis began by a systematic breakdown of the interview into analytic pieces of thought. I rewrote the transcript and, in so doing, analyzed the data line by line, breaking each sentence into incidents, pieces of information, which were then coded. This was a process of identifying and enumerating serially each bit or piece of information whether it seemed relevant or not. The information could have seemed irrelevant to me but relevant for the participant, and I wanted more time with the data before making this distinction. I became thoroughly familiar with the static content and developed an awareness of a pattern or a flow of movement within the data—a process that was slowly evolving. I began to keep memos on a separate page of ideas that might eventually emerge from this information.

☐ *Step 3—Identification and Enumeration of Meaningful Statements:* The purpose of this step was to differentiate those statements with meaningful content relative to the experience of a terminal diagnosis from those statements that were irrelevant, repetitious, or redundant. Each "meaningful statement" was a composite of "incidents" identified in the previous step. When identified, the statement would again be serially enumerated (coded) and the code from Step 2 written at the end of the statement to indicate its source.

APPENDIX

As well as being central to the purpose of the research, the identification of meaningful statements was also pragmatic in that it reduced the number of statements to be incorporated into the description. Related statements were collapsed into one. For purposes of making the content descriptive, first-person pronouns were changed to the third person. This created a sense of distance and objectivity both for myself and for the participant reflecting on the description. Through this shaping process that followed the analytic process, the information was becoming coherent without any change of meaning or loss of information. The number of codes was reduced from 613 in Step 2 to 322 in Step 3.

☐ *Step 4—Clustering of Statements:* This step involved the clustering of certain of the meaningful statements identified in Step 3. These statements, which described different aspects of the participant's experience and at the same time appeared to be related to each other, were shaped into wholes made up of several sentences and were called "clusters."

Until now the process of analysis had been rigorous, time-consuming, and as objective as possible. In contrast, the clustering began on an intuitive level—sentences were grouped together according to their associated meaning. For example, many clusters described Doug Scott's medical history, but each cluster focused on a particular aspect of that history: discovery of illness, action of surgeon, Scott's reactions, Scott's referral, confirmation of the diagnosis. I labeled the clusters with the word most appropriate to its meaning.

By designating each cluster with a conceptual label, I was bringing my interpretation of the participants' experiences into conjunction with that of the participants.

I gradually became aware of underlying patterns and themes. Each cluster had meaning within itself but was also part of a larger mosaic. The incidents had become statements containing a variety of meanings, the statements formed clusters, and the clusters were now differentiated into sections. The data were now in the form of 99 clusters rather than 332 meaningful statements.

☐ *Step 5—Sections:* The clusters originating in Step 4 were developed and organized into five "sections" of interest: (1) diagnoses and reactions, (2) qualities of the individuals themselves, (3) their relationships, (4) the balance point of health or illness, and (5) therapy.

All clusters with labels relating to the topic of diagnosis and reaction were placed in that section. Similarly, all the other clusters were organized according to their topical section. These sections remained constant for each of the six participants with the exception of the fifth section, which required expansion since therapy included many different learning strategies.

These sections paralleled the designated sections of the original interview: (1) diagnosis, (2) activities, (3) relationship and events, (4) meaning of disease, (5) beliefs. This parallel between the sections of the interview and the sections of the analysis seemed to indicate that to some extent the data reflected the nature of the structure of the interview and that the volume and wealth of information elicited resulted in part from the relevance of the interview to the interests and experiences of the participants.

☐ *Step 6—Identification of Categories and Properties:* The clusters were grouped under the five sections of interest or topics listed above. It became evident that within these sections there were different aspects pertaining to particular topics. Accordingly, the clusters were subgrouped, and these subgroupings of different aspects of a topic became the categories. A category is a conceptual element (of the theory) generated by comparative analysis. For example, under the section heading of diagnosis and reaction, there were five different categories or aspects of the diagnosis that emerged from this section of the data: (A) medical information, (B) reaction, (C) acceptance, (D) hopelessness, and (E) personal meaning. Under category B, the data indicated a need for a more extended classification and, therefore, subcategories were created.

Under each of these categories the clusters were now conceived as "properties" or elements of the categories. A property is a conceptual element of a category. Each cluster of properties describes the various elements of the category in which it is classified. Properties are the specific details provided by the individuals which help to indicate the relationship between the conceptual codes.

For example, under Section 1, diagnosis and reaction, is Category B, reaction. A subcategory of reaction is fear. Properties of fear are anxiety, time left to live, fate, and death.

These categories and properties were organized into a sequential pattern, and the developing description then reflected the time sequence of experience reported by the participants.

During the analysis of the five other interviews, the categories remained fairly constant. There were some additions and occasionally some of the categories already named did not emerge. The widest variation occurred in the last section on individual beliefs.

☐ *Step 7—Description:* The last step of Phase One of the analysis was the writing of the description of the experience of each person. The description was developed from the clusters (properties) of the categories. The description was written from the analysis, with the events listed in the time sequence related by the participant. Each participant's language, style, and verbatim expressions were maintained as accurately as possible. Changes were made only to clarify or facilitate the reading of the description. The descriptions were given to each participant for his/her evaluation. With only minor spelling and geographical corrections, the participants approved the integrity of the analysis and descriptions.

After completing Step 5 of the analysis of the second interview, I attempted to fit that data into the categories generated from the first interview. The data fit all but a few categories, emphasizing the common aspects of the experience of terminal illness. The unique aspects were illustrated by the differing properties of the categories but even here there was much agreement. This process of data fit continued throughout the analysis of the six interviews. Some new information initiated new categories, other additional information created more properties. Because of the constant comparative method of analysis and the wealth of meaning, the categories and properties were continually being reshaped. The analysis and description of each of the six interviews produced the data base for Phase Two of the analysis. The material was now organized in such a manner that a representative description could be generated.

☐ THE ANALYSIS: PHASE TWO

Phase Two was more elaborate in that it moved from a rigorously detailed analysis to a representative and theoretical description. It had five purposes: (1) reorganization of preliminary categories and the discovery of representative categories of meaning and their properties, (2) verification and saturation of categories, (3) integration of categories and their properties into themes, (4) discovery of the core category or variable, and (5) development of a substantive theory from the emergence of the core category or basic social process. A description of the first four will comprise the rest of this appendix. The stages of the core category are elucidated in Chapters 4 to 10.

☐ **Step 1—Reorganization of Categories:** The first step was to reorganize the preliminary categories generated from each of the six interviews—to synthesize them into a definitive form. Reorganization was necessary as categories of meaning were now representative of all six participants. They ranged in number from a minimum of thirty-three in one interview to a maximum of forty-six in another. Each category was listed and examined for repetition, overlap, and redundancy.

As additional categories and properties emerged from the data relative to the fifth section, it seemed appropriate to change the heading from "therapy" to "strategies,"; therapy then becoming one of the strategies, that is, a property of that category. It became evident that each individual had developed his or her own strategies for survival and health, thus creating new properties to be categorized. Categories that were not obvious in the initial analysis were now very much in evidence under this section named "strategies." These included fighting, exercise, and spirituality. Two other categories emerged: responsibility and attitude. These categories were eventually subsumed as properties under categories such as individuality, choice, or philosophy. To ensure that no detail of any experience had been overlooked, I went over each individual analysis confirming that each cluster had been assigned to a suitable category. It became clear that all the data fitted into one or another of the categories. The final organization represented thirty-nine categories. Twenty-nine of the categories represented the common experience of all six participants. Six of the remaining categories were representative of the experience of five participants. Four of the categories represented only three participants.

☐ *Step 2—Verification and Saturation:* I found it was necessary not only to accomplish the rigorous coding procedure of Phase One but to go over the data repeatedly in Phase Two, verifying that each meaningful statement was truly related to the cluster in which it was placed and that each cluster was relevant to the category in which it was placed. As the emergent theory was to be grounded in the data, the verification and relevance of the coding were essential. Having expanded or spread the data in the second step of Phase One and in the first step of Phase Two, the procedure now became one of refinement and synthesis.

After repeatedly comparing and analyzing all the categories and properties, I found that sufficient codes had been generated to encompass both different and similar relationships between concepts. The criteria for termination of data collection is the category's "theoretical saturation."[1] This means that very little new information with which to develop properties or increase the understanding of a category is emerging from the data; that is, similar instances are being repeated. This diminution was clearly evident and so no further interviews were needed.

☐ *Step 3—Integration of Categories and Properties into Themes:* At this point I felt it necessary to leave the coded data and take a subjective overview of other sources of information. I decided to read over the memos I had been jotting down throughout the coding process. Glaser describes memos as "the theorizing write-up of ideas about codes and their relationships as they strike the analyst while coding."[2] It is a pragmatic way to store ideas: the ideational development in memos launches the generation of theory. The memos were stimulated by the constant comparative process of juxtaposing property with property and then fitting the property to the relevant category. The memos became the exciting and inspirational part of my investigation. As I read them over, sixteen different, though related, themes emerged. I made an arbitrary decision to do a balance check with what I had written intuitively and subjectively, as memos, against what I had written with as much objectivity and verbatim content as possible—the descrip-

---

[1] Glaser, B. and A. Strauss, *The Discovery of Grounded Theory* (Chicago: Aldine Publishing Co., 1967), p.61.

[2] Glaser, B., *Theoretical Sensitivity* (California: The Sociology Press, 1978), p.83.

tion of the interviews. As I reread each description, I found each of the sixteen memo themes. These themes had emerged from the discovery of the common meaning within the expressed experience of a terminal diagnosis.

☐ *Step 4—Discovery of the Core Category:* The next stage was the discovery of the core category, the base or central meaning of all this information. This was not yet named, yet it related to almost every aspect of the analysis: hence it's descriptive adjective "core."

For the purpose of verifying this core category that was emerging from the themes, I reread again each individual description. I then wrote a brief paragraph summarizing my interpretation of its essential meaning. Each summarization was a variation on the subject I have chosen to call "Personal Agency." The criteria I used to select Personal Agency as the core category were suggested by Glaser.

In this study, the theoretical code is a process termed by Glaser "a basic social process." The distinction between a basic social process and one that remains only as a core category is that the former has two or more emergent stages. In fact, Personal Agency has seven stages. A description of how the six participants in this study confronted their terminal illness and became active agents in affirming their lives and their health is given in Chapters 4 to 10.

☐ References

Achterberg, J., O. Carl Simonton, and S. Matthews-Simonton, *Stress, Psychological Factors and Cancer.* Fort Worth: New Medicine Press, 1976.

Allport, G. "Preface." In V. Frankl, *Man's Search for Meaning.* New York: Simon and Schuster, 1959.

Assagioli, R. *Psychosynthesis.* New York: Viking Press, 1965.

Assagioli, R. *Act of Will.* New York: Penguin Books, 1974.

Bahnson, C. Second Conference on Psychophysiological Aspects of Cancer. *Annals of the New York Academy of Sciences* 164, (1969): 307–634.

Bahnson, C. and D. Kissen. Conference on Psychophysiological Aspects of Cancer. *Annals of the New York Academy of Sciences* 125 (1966): 773–1055.

Bailar, John C. "Mammography: A Contrary View." *Annals of Internal Medicine,* vol. 84, no. 1, January 1976: 77–84.

Barnett, L. *The Universe and Dr. Einstein.* New York: Mentor Books, 1948.

Bateson, G. *Steps to an Ecology of Mind.* New York: Ballantine Books, 1972.

——— *Mind and Nature: A Necessary Unity.* New York: E.P. Dutton, 1979.

Beecher, H. "The Powerful Placebo." *Journal of the American Medical Association* 176 (1961): 1102.

Bigus, O., S. Hadden, and B. Glaser. "The Study of Basic Social Processes." In R. Smith and P. Manning (Eds.) *The Handbook of Social Science Methods: Qualitative Methods.* New York: Irvington Publishers, 1979.

Blumberg, E., P. West, and F. Ellis. "A Possible Relationship Between Psychological Factors and Human Cancer." *Psychosomatic Medicine* 16(4) (1954): 276–86.

Bogdan, R. and S. Taylor. *Introduction to Qualitative Research.* Toronto: John Wiley & Sons, 1975.

Bohm, D. *Fragmentation and Wholeness.* The Van Leer Foundation, 1976.

Booth, G. "Health from the Standpoint of the Physician." In P.B. Manes (Ed.) *The Church and Mental Health.* New York: Scribner, 1953.

——— "Introduction." In A. Siirala, *The Voice of Illness.* New York: Edwin Mellen Press, 1964.

——— "The Prevention and Cure of Cancer." An address published by the National Federation of Spiritual Healers Research. Manchester, England, May 1972.

——— *The Cancer Epidemic: Shadow of the Conquest of Nature.* New York: Edwin Mellen Press, 1979.

Brown, B. *New Mind, New Body.* New York: Harper & Row, 1975.

Bruyn, S. *The Human Perspective in Sociology: The Methodology of Participant Observation.* New Jersey: Prentice Hall, 1966.

Buber, M. *The Knowledge of Man.* New York: Harper & Row, 1965.

Campbell, J. *The Hero with a Thousand Faces.* Princeton, N.J.: Princeton University Press, 1949.

Cannon, W. *The Wisdom of the Body.* New York: W.W. Norton & Co., 1932.

Capra, F. *The Tao of Physics.* Great Britain: Richard Clay (The Chaucer Press), 1975.

Colaizzi, P. *Reflection and Research in Psychology: A Phenomenological Study of Learning.* Dubuque: Kendall/Hunt Publishing Co., 1973.

——— "Learning and Existence." In R. Valle & M. King (Eds.) *Existential-Phenomenological Perspectives for Psychology.* Toronto: Oxford University Press, 1978.

Cousins, N. "Anatomy of an Illness or One Chance in 500 to Live." *Saturday Review* 4 (May 28), 1977.

——— "The Mysterious Placebo." *Saturday Review* 5 (October 1), 1977.

——— *Anatomy of an Illness.* New York: W.W. Norton & Co., 1979.

REFERENCES

Crampton, M. "The Use of Mental Imagery in Pscyhosynthesis." *Journal of Humanistic Psychology* (Fall), 1969.

Cunningham, A.J. "Mind, Body and Immune Response." In Adler, R. (Ed.) *Psychoneuroimmunology.* New York: Academic Press, 1981.

Day, S. *Cancer, Stress and Death.* New York: Plenum, 1979.

Dilthey, W. *Dilthey: Selected Writings* (H. Rickman, ed.) London: Cambridge University Press, 1976.

Dubos, R. *Mirage of Health.* New York: Harper & Row, 1959.

—— "Introduction." In N. Cousins, *Anatomy of an Illness.* New York: W.W. Norton & Co., 1979.

English, H. and A. English. *A Comprehensive Dictionary of Psychological and Psychoanalytical Terms.* New York: David McKay Co., 1958.

Erickson, E. *Childhood and Society.* New York: W.W. Norton & Co., 1963.

Evans, D. Struggle and Fulfillment. New York: Wm. Collins Publishers, 1979.

Evans, E. *A Psychological Study of Cancer.* New York: Dodd, Mead & Co., 1926.

Ferguson, M. *The Aquarian Conspiracy.* Los Angeles: J.P. Tarcher, 1980.

Frankl, V. *Man's Search for Meaning.* New York: Simon & Schuster, 1959.

Freud, S. *A General Introduction to Psychoanalysis.* New York: Permabooks, 1956.

Friedman, M. *Martin Buber: The Life of Dialogue.* New York: Harper & Row, 1960.

—— *The Hidden Human Image.* New York: Dell Publishing Co., 1974.

—— "Healing Through Meeting: A Dialogical Approach to Psychotherapy." Parts I and II. *The American Journal of Psychoanalysis* 35 (1975); 255–67, 343–54.

Fromm, E. *Man for Himself.* New York: Rinehart & Co., 1947.

Giorgi, A. *Psychology as a Human Science.* New York: Harper & Row, 1970.

—— "Convergence and Divergence of Qualitative and Quantitive Methods in Psychology." In A. Giorgi, C. Fisher, and E. Murray (Eds.) *Duquesne Studies in Phenomenological Psychology.* Vol. II. Pittsburgh: Duquesne University Press, 1975.

Glaser, B. *Theoretical Sensitivity.* California: The Sociology Press, 1978.

Glaser, B. and A. Strauss. *The Discovery of Grounded Theory.* Chicago: Aldine Publishing Co., 1967.

Glasser, R. *The Body is the Hero.* New York: Random House, 1976.

Green, E. and A. Green. *Beyond Biofeedback.* New York: Delcorte, 1977.

Hinsie, L. and R. Campbell. *Psychiatric Dictionary.* New York: Oxford University Press, 1970.

Holmes, I. and R. Rahe. "The Social Readjustment Rating Scale." *Journal of Psychosomatic Research* 11 (1967): 213–18. Pergamon Journals Ltd.

Horney, K. *Neurosis and Human Growth.* New York: W.W. Norton & Co., 1950.

Hunt, D. "The New Three R's in Person-Environment Interaction: Responsiveness, Reciprocality and Reflexivity," *Dutch Educational Journal of Research* 4 (1979): 184–90.

Hutschnecker, A. *The Will to Live.* New York: Thomas Y. Crowell Company, 1953.

Huxley, J. "Introduction." In P. Teilhard de Chardin, *The Phenomenon of Man.* New York: Harper & Row, 1959.

Illich, I. *Limits of Medicine.* London: Calder & Boyars, 1976.

——*Medical Nemesis.* London: Calder & Boyars, 1975.

Jaffe, D. *Healing from Within.* New York: Bantam Books, 1980.

Jaffe, D. and C. Scott. *From Burnout to Balance.* New York: McGraw-Hill, 1984.

James, W. *Principles of Psychology* (2 vols.). New York: Holt, Rinehart & Winston, 1890.

Jantsch, E. *The Self-Organizing Universe.* New York: Pergamon Press, 1979.

Joy, W. Brugh. *Joy's Way.* Los Angeles: J.P. Tarcher, 1979.

Jung, C. *Memories, Dreams and Reflections.* New York: Vintage, 1961.

Kavetsky, R., N. Turkevitch, and K. Balitsky. "On the Psychophysiological Mechanism of the Organism's Resistance to Tumor Growth." Annals of the New York Academy of Sciences 125 (1966): 933–45.

Keen, E. *Psychology and the New Consciousness.* Belmont: Wadsworth Publishing Co., 1972.

REFERENCES

―― *A Primer in Phenomenological Psychology*. Toronto: Holt, Rinehart & Winston, 1975.

―― "Part Two: The unique event." Unpublished manuscript. *Proceedings of the Annual Convention of the Association of Humanistic Psychology*. Princeton, August 1979.

Keen, S. "The Myths We Live and Die By." *New Age* 4:11 (May 1979), pp. 30–32.

Kelly, G. *The Psychology of Personal Constructs*. New York: Norton, 1955.

Kimble, G. and N. Garmezy. *Principles of General Psychology*. 2nd ed. New York: Ronald, 1963.

King, Vivian. "Embracing Disease." Pamphlet. Pasadena, California: Pschosynthesis Training Center, 1983.

Kissen, D. "The Significance of Personality in Lung Cancer in Men." *Annals of the New York Academy of Sciences* 125 (1966): 820—26.

Koestler, A. *Janus*. New York: Random House, 1978.

Kripalu Yoga Fellowship. "How to Give Yourself a Massage." *The Self-Health Guide: A Personal Program for Holistic Living*. Kripalu Center for Holistic Health, copyright 1980.

Krippner, S. and A. Villoldo. *The Realms of Healing*. California: Celestial Arts, 1976.

Kubler-Ross, E. *On Death and Dying*. New York: Macmillan Publishing Co., 1969.

La Barba, R. "Experiential and Environmental Factors in Cancer. A Review of Research." *Psychosomatic Medicine* 32 (1970): 259–76.

LeShan, L. "An Emotional Life History Pattern Associated with Neoplastic Disease. *Annals of the New York Academy of Sciences* 125 (1966): 780–93.

―― "Mobilizing the Life Force." *Annals of the New York Academy of Sciences* 164 (1969): 847–61.

―― *You Can Fight for Your Life*. New York: M. Evans & Co., 1977.

LeShan, L. and R. Worthington. "Some Psychological Correlates of Neoplastic Diesease: A Preliminary Report," *Journal of Clinical Experimental Psychopathology* 16 (1955): 281–88.

―― "Personality as a Factor in the Pathogenesis of Cancer: A Review of the Literature." *British Journal of Medical Psychology* 29 (1956): 49–56.

Lockhart, R. "Cancer in Myth and Dream." *Spring* 1 (1977): 1–26, Zurich.

Maslow, A. *Motivation and Personality*. New York: Harper & Row, 1954.

―― *Toward a Psychology of Being*. New York: Van Nostrand, 1962.

―― *The Psychology of Science*. Chicago: Henry Regnery Co., 1966.

May, R. *Man's Search for Himself*. New York: Dell Publishing Co., 1953.

―― *Existence: A New Dimension in Psychiatry and Psychology*. New York: Simon & Schuster, 1958.

―― *Psychology and the Human Dilemma*. Toronto: Van Nostrand Reinhold, 1966.

―― *Love and Will*. New York: Dell Publishing Co., 1969.

McKeown, T. *The Role of Medicine. Dream, Mirage or Nemesis*. Princeton, N.J.: Princeton University Press, 1979.

Mendelsohn, Robert S. *Confessions of a Medical Heretic*. New York: Warner Books, 1979.

Moser, R. *Diseases of Medical Progress: A Study of Iatrogenic Disease*. Springfield, Illinois: Charles C. Thomas, 1969.

Moustakas, C. (Ed.). *The Self. Explorations in Personal Growth*. New York: Harper & Row, 1956.

―― "Heuristic Research." In *Individuality and Encounter*. Cambridge, Mass.: H.A. Doyle Publishing Co., 1968.

―― *Loneliness and Love*. New York: Prentice-Hall, Spectrum, 1972.

Muse, M. *A Textbook of Psychology*. Philadelphia: Saunders, 1939.

Pelletier, K. *Mind as Healer, Mind as Slayer*. New York: Dell Publishing Co., 1977.

Platt, John. "The Future of AIDS." In *The Futurist*, vol. XXI, no.6, November–December 1987.

Polanyi, M. *Personal Knowledge*. Chicago: University of Chicago Press, 1958.

―― *The Tacit Dimension*. New York: Doubleday & Co., 1966.

Prigogine, I. *From Being to Becoming*. San Francisco: W.H. Freeman and Co., 1980.

Read, H. *Education Through Art*. New York: Pantheon Books, 1958.

REFERENCES

Riley, V. "Mouse Mammary Tumors: Alteration of Incidence as Apparent Function of Stress." *Science* 189 (1975): 465–67.

Robinson, M. "Visual Imagery, Bioenergetics and the Treatment of Cancer." Paper presented at the Third International Bioenergetic Conference at Waterville Valley, New Hampshire, July 25 to August 1, 1976. Published later in *Bioenergetics*, January 1978.

Roffers, M. "How to Fight Cancer with Your Fork." *Medical Self-Care*. September–October, 1985.

Rogers, Carl. *On Becoming a Person*. Boston: Houghton Mifflin, 1961.

Rosenthall, R. *Experimenter Effects in Behavioral Research*. New York: Appleton-Century-Crofts, 1966.

Schmale, A. and H. Iker, "The Psychological Setting of Uterine Cervical Cancer." *Annals of the New York Academy of Sciences* 125 (1966): 807–13.

—— "Hopelessness as a Predictor of Cervical Cancer. *Social Science and Medicine* 5 (1971): 95–100.

Seligman, M. *Helplessness. On Depression, Development and Death*. San Francisco: W.H. Freeman & Co., 1975.

Selye, H. *The Physiology and Pathology of Exposure to Stress*. Montreal: Acta, 1950.

—— *The Stress of Life*. New York: McGraw-Hill, 1956.

—— *Stress Without Distress*. Toronto, New American Library, 1975.

—— *From Dream to Discovery*. New York: Arno Press, 1964.

—— *The Stress of My Life*. Toronto: McClelland & Stewart, 1977.

Shapiro, A. "Factors Contributing to the Placebo Effect." *American Journal of Psychotherapy* 19 (1961): 73–88.

Shotter, J. *Images of Man in Psychological Research*. London: Richard Clay, 1975.

Simonton Tapes. *Psychological Factors, Stress and Cancer*. Simonton, O. Carl and S. Matthews-Simonton. Fort Worth: Texas. Cancer Counseling and Research Center, 1976.

Simonton, O. Carl and S. Matthews-Simonton, "Belief Systems and Management of the Emotional Aspects of Malignancy." *Journal of Transpersonal Psychology* 7 (1975): 29–48.

Simonton O. Carl, S. Matthews-Simonton, and J. Creighton. *Getting Well Again*. Toronto: Bantam Books, 1980.

Simonton, O. Carl, S. Matthews-Simonton, and C. Sparks. "Psychological Intervention in the Treatment of Cancer." *Psychosomatics* 21(3) (1980): 226–33.

Siirala, A. *The Voice of Illness. A Study in Therapy and Prohpecy* (1st ed., 1964). Toronto/New York: Edwin Mellen Press, 1981.

——— "Some Implications for Hermeneutics of the Anthropological Medicine Developed by Viktor Von Weizaecker." An address given to the American Academy of Religion in Dallas, Texas, 1981.

Skinner, B. *Science and Human Behavior.* New York: Macmillan, 1953.

Snow, J. *Clinical Notes on Cancer.* London: J.& A. Churchill, 1883; *Cancer and Cancer Process,* 1893.

Solomon, G., R. Amkraut, and P. Kasper. "Immunity, Emotions and Stress." *Annals of Clinical Research* 6 (1974): 313–22.

Teilhard de Chardin, P. *The Phenomenon of Man.* New York: Harper & Row, 1959.

Thomas, C. and D. Duszynski. "Closeness to Parents and Family Constellation in a Prospective Study of Five Disease States: Suicide, Mental Illness, Malignant Tumor, Hypertension, and Coronary Heart Disease. *The John Hopkins Medical Journal* 134 (1974): 251–70.

Tiger, L. *Optimism: The Biology of Hope.* New York: Simon & Schuster, 1979.

Tillich, P. *The Courage To Be.* Connecticut: Yale University Press, 1952.

Tinbergen, N. "Etiology and Stress Diseases." *Science* 185 (1974): 26.

Walshe, W. *Nature and Treatment of Cancer.* London: Taylor & Walton, 1846.

Webster's New Collegiate Dictionary. Toronto: Thomas Allen & Son, 1979.

Wrightsman, L., C. Sigelman, and F. Sanford. *Psychology: A Scientific Study of Human Behavior.* California: Brooks/Cole Publishing Co., 1961.

Wundt, W. "Contributions to the Theory of Sensory Perception." In T. Shipley (Ed.) *Classics in Psychology,* 51–78. New York: Philosophical Library, 1961.

CPSIA information can be obtained at www.ICGtesting.com
Printed in the USA
LVOW071152230911

247551LV00001B/86/A